THE TWO FAT LADIES
RIDE AGAIN

THE TWO FAT LADIES
RIDE AGAIN

Jennifer Paterson and
Clarissa Dickson Wright

Clarkson Potter/Publishers
New York

NOTE: ALL RECIPES SERVE 4 UNLESS OTHERWISE STATED

DEDICATION

Jennifer dedicates her part in this book to Milo Parmoor, "my friend of long-lasting years." Clarissa dedicates her part in this book to "my beloved director and friend, Pat Llewellyn" and to Angus Hamilton, whose kind gift made writing it a pleasure.

Text copyright © 1997 by Optomen Television and Jennifer Paterson and Clarissa Dickson Wright
Photographs copyright © 1997 by Ebury Press or Optomen Television

Published by Clarkson N. Potter, Inc., 201 East 50th Street, New York, New York 10022.
Member of the Crown Publishing Group.

Random House, Inc. New York, Toronto, London, Sydney, Auckland

www.randomhouse.com

CLARKSON POTTER, POTTER, and colophon are trademarks of Clarkson N. Potter, Inc.

Originally published in Great Britain by Ebury Press in 1997.

Printed in Portugal

Library of Congress Cataloging-in-Publication Data is available upon request.

ISBN 0-609-60379-5

10 9 8 7 6 5 4 3 2 1

First American Edition

CONTENTS

ACKNOWLEDGMENTS

We would like to thank all the following:

Patricia Llewellyn, our Welsh witch, who invented us and continues to put up with us, and who looks too young to be so clever.

Peter Gillbe, who continues to strive and negotiate so shrewdly on our behalf.

Steven Surbey, who has won his spurs and become our most brilliant researcher, so that Jennifer cannot have him to herself any more.

Gerry MacMahon, our new researcher, whose personal charms and Irish blarney open every door.

Rex Philips, our darling Rex, without whom we would be desolate and without any voice. May he never leave us.

Saint Luke Cardiff, who turns out to be a brilliant croquet player as well as a dab hand with the camera, and his assistant Louis Caulfield, with whom Clarissa has an on-going pool championship.

Darling Spike Geilinger, our other cameraman, as suave as ever.

Paul Ratcliffe, without whose editing and post-production skills, our beloved director would probably spin into orbit.

Lisa Andreae, who watches the pennies – yea, even to the cannon's mouth!

Polly Livingston, production co-ordinator, who has greatly improved the standard of food we get on location this time, and who works ceaselessly for our well-being.

Elaine Walker (Clarissa's "visagist") and Vicky Watts, who has the unholy task of co-ordinating the cooking shots, the new bods this year.

The long-suffering crowd at Ebury Press, Fiona MacIntyre and Penny Simpson, and our copy editor, Norma Macmillan.

Jason Bell for his brilliant cover photograph.

Pete Smith and Virginia Alcock for their tireless efforts and wonderful food styling.

Mark Thompson and Adam Kemp at BBC2 for continuing to believe in us.

And all the other splendid people who have helped us in our travels.

The recipe for Cheese Soufflé Tartlets on page 149 is taken from Margaret Costa's *Four Season's Cookery Book* (Grub Street 1997) and is reproduced by kind permission of the publishers.

INTRODUCTION

Pat Llewellyn directs the Ladies at the Devil's Bridge at Kirkby Lonsdale, Cumbria

"Are you the other fat lady?" I was asked at a party last year, a few months before our first program was transmitted. I am rather relieved that the popularity of the series means such incidences of mistaken identity no longer occur. I do not have Clarissa's talent for the witty riposte. "Don't you find the title of the series rather offensive?" one journalist asked her. "We don't mind 'Two', and there's nothing wrong with 'Fat'," replied Clarissa, "but we don't like 'Ladies'. It makes us sound like a public convenience."

The popularity of "Two Fat Ladies" and the celebrity it brought Clarissa and Jennifer have been a tremendous thrill for those of us who made the series. We were delighted that enthusiastic viewers actually bothered to write in and when the first few appreciative letters arrived at the office, we read them aloud with pride.

Then the sackfuls arrived. Women wrote saying that their husbands had ventured into the kitchen for the first time after seeing the program. One said that the program had saved her marriage (we were fascinated, but unfortunately she did not elaborate).

Many people were curious to know if Clarissa and Jennifer were really as they seemed on television. If anything, they are a little more toned down on screen than they are in the flesh. There are many conversations we have filmed on location that have hit the cutting room floor for fear of a public outcry or a costly libel suit.

Everyone asks what they are like to work with. It would be dishonest to say that it was always easy. A tight budget and a large film crew can be a tricky equation to reckon with on location, particularly when your crew includes two loud-voiced, bold-spirited presenters who are rather intolerant of bad cooking and do not believe in that rather English habit of never complaining.

"What on earth have they put in this sauce?" boomed Clarissa to her co-presenter from the far end of the table during our first evening on location at one hotel restaurant. The whole restaurant seemed to pause for Jennifer's reply. She slowly chewed on her scallop without any hint of enjoyment. "I think it must be glue," she concluded.

There have been other occasions when I have wished I was somewhere else. After the first series was broadcast, we were invited to lunch by a BBC supremo. Such occasions are rare. My feeble attempts to explain to Clarissa and Jennifer the importance of the meeting were met with the usual mischievous giggles. After pleading with them on the way to the restaurant to behave, I watched with silent, squirming anxiety as they sat each side of the controller of BBC2 (and controller of our future), passing the end of his tie across the table, teasing him about the design, and prodding his tummy when he said he was on a diet. Clarissa wanted to see his calves (she has what might be described as a fetish for

men's legs) and Jennifer, stroking his head gently, wanted to know how old he was. "You look too young for such a grand job," she announced.

But the penalties of these embarrassing experiences are small beer compared to what I have gained from working with them. I enjoy an enormous professional respect from Jennifer and Clarissa. But more than that, I have found two incredibly good and loyal friends in spite of our odd mixture of ages, beliefs and backgrounds. Clarissa is at the ready to defend me at the slightest disagreement with a boss, parent or plumber ("Give me the phone number, I'll speak to them"). Jennifer proffers lots of sensible advice when it comes to love and relationships ("What is that garment you're wearing. You'll never find a husband wearing that!").

I know that for Clarissa and Jennifer fat is not a feminist issue ("Feminists? Ghastly women with terrible clothes") and neither of them would relish the idea that they might be characterised as role models for women trying to forge a career in television ("They should learn to cook – far more useful when they get married than hanging around in television studios.") But in an industry where women's success in front of the camera is mostly defined by youthful good looks and anodyne personalities, Jennifer and Clarissa's success is an enormous achievement.

Patricia Llewellyn
Producer

LIGHT DISHES, APPETIZERS, AND SAVORIES

At the classic motorcycle rally in Hesket Newmarket, Jennifer and

Clarissa admire the bikes

CLARISSA WRITES: The publishers in all their wisdom have headed this section "Light Dishes, Appetizers, and Savories" so you will get all confused, but in ten years of bookselling I have found they never take the easy path. The comparable program in the series is lunch, so that is what I shall talk about.

Jennifer loves lunches. She says they are the first event of the day, when everyone is fresh and full of joie de vivre, as opposed to dinner when people may be a little tired. Lunch parties during the week, she says, feel deeply wicked, as they are more usually held at weekends. If you really want to delight Jennifer take her to the cinema afterwards, particularly in fine weather: she says

there is something deeply immoral about going into a darkened cinema when the sun is shining. I wish my own sense of illicit pleasure was so easily and innocently attained.

Lunch came very late into the historic scene. In the days when people's lives were governed by the sun, breakfast was taken at dawn, dinner as the main meal of the day began in summer at 10am and in winter at noon, supper was taken before bed and that was it. Gradually dinner was eaten later and later, and as the quality of artificial light sources improved, it became an evening meal. It is interesting that the Americans, who still uphold many eighteenth-century customs, eat their evening meal much earlier than

*A stroll through the village of Hesket Newmarket
before cooking lunch*

Savories are an extra course taken at dinner after the pudding, beloved by men. If you want to keep your paramour or even your husband happy, give him a savory from time to time.

For the program we gave Jennifer a treat and cooked lunch at a classic motorcycle rally at Hesket Newmarket in Cumbria. What fun we had belting round the lanes surrounded by charming men on beautiful bikes, and how heartily they devoured our offerings.

we do. As dinner moved to later in the day, a gap appeared. In the late Middle Ages there was a meal called nuncheon which corresponded roughly with our elevenses, and by late Georgian times this had developed into luncheon, which was indeed a light meal taken at midday, with dinner at the daring hour of five or even (oh so modern!) six o'clock.

Today we do not rise in summer until it has been light for hours and with a reckless disregard for the daylight clock we sit up half the night and dine at 8 o'clock or even later. Lunch has therefore become a very necessary midday repast. A whole luncheon culture has grown up among rich, elegant women who sit around in couture dresses and good jewellery, gossiping and picking at salad lest they destroy their anorexic figures. The late Duchess of Windsor left many sad legacies, but none as detrimental to human enjoyment as her comment that "one can never be too rich or too thin."

*Some of the grateful recipients of lunch cooked by
Jennifer and Clarissa*

Crème Vichyssoise Glacée

To my mind this is one of the most delicious of iced soups. It was invented in New York in 1917 by Louis Diat, the French chef des cuisines at the Ritz-Carlton. As we can now get leeks all year round this makes a very suitable soup for a lovely summer's day, either at home or taken on a picnic in a sturdy thermos flask.

Serves 8

6 good-size leeks
4 tablespoons (½ stick) unsalted butter
6 medium potatoes, peeled and finely sliced
5 cups chicken stock or water
salt and freshly ground pepper
¾ cup heavy cream
fresh chives

Trim the leeks and slice the white parts very finely (you can use the green parts in a fry-up with new potatoes – very good). Melt the butter in a saucepan large enough to contain all the ingredients and stew the leeks until softish. Add the potatoes and stir to mix with the leeks. Pour in the stock or water and season with salt. Bring to the boil, then simmer for 40 minutes.

Allow to cool a little, then whizz the whole lot in a blender until smooth working in batches as necessary. Cool, then stir in the cream. Check the seasoning, adding some freshly ground pepper. Chill thoroughly for about 6 hours or overnight. Serve in nice little bowls with snipped chives sprinkled on top.

JP

Garlic Soup with Poached Eggs

Every food writer bangs on about the Mediterranean and Levantine civilisations' use of garlic, but turn to Skeat's *Etymological Dictionary* and there it is: garlic: Anglo-Saxon spearleek from gar, a spear. What, I wonder, did the Anglo-Saxons do with garlic that they took the trouble to name it? We are so brainwashed with information about the diet of bronzed southern peasants nowadays that we overlook our own heritage. Yet on my morning walks the riverbank is rank with the smell of wild garlic, and as I pick the flowers and take them home to adorn my salads I think how glad our ancestors must have been to see the herb after the long winter days with no greenery in sight. This recipe is one to set the blood coursing through your veins, to burn away the last vestigial mists and lingering viruses of winter and enable you to greet the Spring as sexually aroused as the Ayuvedics and Macrobiotics fear you will be if you eat this splendid herb.

2 thick slices of country-style bread, crusts removed
4 garlic cloves, finely chopped
2 tablespoons olive oil
1 teaspoon paprika
4 cups chicken stock
4 eggs
salt

Preheat the oven to 325°F.

In a flameproof casserole fry the bread with the garlic in the oil until golden. When you turn the bread slices, sprinkle on the paprika. Remove to a blender or food processor and purée with a little of the stock.

Return to the casserole. Add the remaining stock and bring to the boil.

Break the eggs into four ovenproof soup plates. Pour in the soup.

Cook in the oven for 6–8 minutes, until the eggs are set.

CDW

Clarissa's Clam Chowder

In the days when I cooked on a yacht out of Newport Rhode Island, I was constantly struck by how dull clam chowder is. Last year my friend Moira Elias asked me to cook a traditional Thanksgiving Dinner for twenty-four people, starting with clam chowder. Depressed by this thought I was sitting in my beloved Valvonna and Crolla having breakfast when I had a flash of inspiration. I rushed to their charcuterie counter and bought a heel of some speck di prosciutto and a small piece of bacon from pigs raised on chestnuts. The resulting dish was such a success that the mother of the bride for Edinburgh's smartest wedding last year requested my clam chowder and nothing else for her daughter's pre-wedding family lunch.

2 pints fresh clams or canned clams
½ pound speck di prosciutto or other interesting bacon, cut into small pieces
3 small onions, finely diced
3 cups boiling water
1½ pounds potatoes, peeled and diced
a pinch of freshly ground black pepper
3 cups milk

If using fresh clams, shuck them (open the shells with a strong, blunt-ended knife and remove the clams), or steam them open using a little white wine. Keep all the liquor from the shells too.

In a heavy frying pan slowly fry the bacon and onions until golden; transfer to a saucepan. Add the boiling water, potatoes and pepper, and simmer for about 15 minutes or until potatoes are tender. Add the fresh or canned clams, with their liquor, and the milk. Bring to the boil and cook for 5 minutes, then remove from the heat and allow to sit for 1 hour.

Just before serving, reheat the chowder. Ladle into bowls over crumbled crackers. (You can get rid of a lot of anger by putting your packets of crackers in a plastic bag and throwing them on the floor repeatedly, until they reach the required state of crumb. Or stamp on them, says my friend Claire Macdonald, shrieking at British Telecom with each stamp.)

CDW

Bahaian Crab Soup

I have always had a fondness for crabs, and where I live I can get live crabs from my beloved fishmonger, David Clark of Fisherrow. The crabs of the Brazilian Atlantic Coast are similar to our own, and in Brazil they use them to make a deliciously spicy soup.

3 good sized crabs, such as Dungeness, or 2 pounds cooked crab meat
2 onions, chopped
2 garlic cloves, finely chopped
2 tablespoons olive oil
1 celery stalk, chopped
2 large tomatoes, peeled, seeded and chopped
1 hot chile pepper, seeded and chopped
1 tablespoon chopped parsley
2 tablespoons chopped fresh cilantro, plus extra to garnish
1 tablespoon chopped fresh basil
1 13½-ounce can coconut milk
6 limes
salt and freshly ground pepper

Cook your crabs and pick out all the meat. Put the shells in a saucepan, add some of the chopped onion and garlic, and cover with water. Simmer for 20 minutes. Strain and reserve 5 cups of this stock. (If you are using crab meat, and have no shells, substitute fish stock for the crab shell stock.)

Heat the oil in a heavy saucepan, add the remaining onions and garlic and the celery, and fry for 5 minutes to soften. Add the tomatoes and chile and cook for another 5 minutes, stirring frequently. Add the parsley, cilantro, basil and stock. Bring to the boil and simmer for 15 minutes. Add the crab meat, coconut milk and the juice of 3 of the limes. Season well, then heat through. Serve garnished with a little chopped cilantro and slices of lime.

CDW

Steamed Salmon in Lettuce Leaves with Egg and Lemon Sauce

Here is a very dainty dish to set before anyone, let alone a king.

one 8–10-ounce salmon steak
8–10 lettuce leaves (not outside manky ones)
salt and freshly ground pepper
a few drops of lemon juice
2 tablespoons (¼ stick) butter

FOR THE SAUCE:
2 egg yolks
4 tablespoons lemon juice
½ tablespoon butter
1 teaspoon chopped fresh chives
salt and freshly ground pepper

Remove the skin and bones from the salmon steak. This will leave you with two fingers of salmon from each. Slice each finger through the middle to make four fingers. Place the skin and bones in a saucepan with 1 cup of water. Bring to a boil and simmer gently for 20 minutes. Strain and reserve for the sauce. Blanch the lettuce leaves for a second or two in boiling salted water and pat dry. Take two lettuce leaves and spread them out, slightly overlapping. Place a salmon finger on top and sprinkle with salt, pepper and one or two drops of lemon juice. Add ½ tablespoon of butter. Wrap the lettuce around the salmon, then gently squeeze the parcel into a roll. Make three more parcels in the same way.

To make the sauce, whisk the egg yolks in a bowl and gradually beat in the lemon juice. Pour into a small saucepan, add 2 tablespoons of the reserved fish stock and whisk over a low heat until the sauce thickens. Do not boil. Whisk in the butter and chopped chives and season to taste. Keep the sauce warm.

Steam the salmon parcels over simmering water for about 10 minutes. Place each parcel on a plate, cut in half at an angle and pour a little sauce around each.

JP

Squid Tempura

This method of dealing with squid ensures that it is tender. Squid is tough only when overcooked.

1½ pounds squid (body only), cleaned

oil for deep frying

lemon quarters

salt

FOR THE BATTER:

2 large egg yolks

2 cups ice water

2 cups all-purpose flour

FOR THE DIPPING SAUCE:

1 cup fish stock or water

4 tablespoons soy sauce

4 tablespoons mirin (sweet rice wine)

Cut the squid bodies into rings, and reserve.

Unlike most batters, the one for tempura should be made immediately before using. Put the egg yolks in a bowl and beat lightly. Add the ice water and again beat lightly. Add the flour all at once and stir briefly, just enough to combine. Do not worry if the batter is slightly lumpy.

Dredge the squid pieces in the batter, shake off excess and deep fry in very hot oil for 1–2 minutes or until golden brown all over. Remove from the oil and drain on paper towels. Do not cook too many pieces of squid at once, and don't let the oil temperature drop too much or the batter will be greasy and soggy.

While the tempura fries, heat the dipping sauce ingredients in a saucepan to boiling point, then reduce the heat to keep the sauce warm until ready to serve. A little shredded fresh ginger root and grated Japanese radish (daikon) may be added to the sauce.

The squid is served on individual plates with lemon wedges, plenty of salt and the dipping sauce.

JP

Illustrated overleaf

Paulista Cuzcuz

This recipe from Brazil (a native of São Paulo is called a Paulista) was given to my mother by a splendid woman named Dorothy Russell who once jumped into a swimming pool – riding boots, breeches and all – to save me from drowning. The Brazilians make their Cuzcuz from a mixture of cassava flour and flaky corn flour, which I give in this recipe, but I tend to use all ordinary semolina couscous, moistened with stock and set aside to swell while I make the shrimp mixture.

1½ pounds medium shrimps
2 cups untoasted cassava flour
(also called tapioca flour or meal)
1 pound flaky stoneground
corn flour
5 cups fish stock, preferably
home-made, or made with fish
bouillon cubes
1 tablespoon dried shrimps or
Indonesian shrimp paste
(available at Asian groceries)
¾ cup frozen petite peas
4 tablespoons vegetable or
peanut oil
2 onions, grated
5 tomatoes, peeled, seeded
and chopped
⅓ cup black olives, pitted
and chopped
2 scallions, chopped
1 7.75-ounce can hearts of
palm, drained and chopped
salt and freshly ground pepper
1 4½-ounce can sardines, filleted
a bunch of parsley, chopped
5 kale or collard leaves,
center rib removed

Peel the shrimps (use the heads and shells to make the fish stock). Keep 6 shrimps whole and chop the rest. Set aside.

Combine the cassava flour and corn flour. Add the stock and work in until the mixture is smooth - it should not be too dry. Set aside. Pound the dried shrimps finely. Cook the peas in a little hot water very briefly, then drain.

Heat the oil in a heavy pan and fry the onions until they soften and are golden brown. Add the tomatoes and dried shrimps and cook a little longer, stirring. Mix this into the cassava mixture together with the olives, peas, scallions, chopped shrimps, hearts of palm and parsley. Season well. Add more stock if the mixture is too dry.

Oil a small colander (about 9 inches across) and sprinkle with water. Line the colander with the sardines and the reserved whole shrimps. Spoon the cassava mixture into the colander, packing it down gently. Cover with the kale leaves and seal tightly with aluminum foil. Set over a saucepan of simmering water and steam for 30–35 minutes. Let the Cuzcuz rest for 10 minutes, then turn out and serve.

CDW

Janssen's Temptation

Janssen was a well-known(ish) opera singer who famously made this dish for his friends after a night on the town. The ingredients were all he had in his larder. Today, his recipe is better known than his music.

Serves 6 as an appetizer, or
4 as a light lunch

5 large potatoes
1 large onion, sliced
2 tablespoons vegetable oil
4 tablespoons (½ stick) butter
2 tins anchovy fillets, drained
salt and freshly ground
white pepper
2 rounded tablespoons white
bread crumbs
2½ cups heavy cream
4 tablespoons milk

Peel the potatoes and cut into strips a little thicker than matchsitcks. Keep the strips of potato in cold water so that they do not discolor (when ready to use, drain and pat dry with paper towels). Fry the onion gently in the oil and ½ tablespoon butter until soft.

Preheat the oven to 400°F.

Arrange a layer of potato strips in a buttered gratin dish, then add a layer of onion and anchovies. Sprinkle with a little salt and pepper, then add another layer of potato and so on, continuing until the ingredients are finished. Sprinkle the bread crumbs over the top and dot with the remaining 3½ tablespoons butter. Heat the cream and milk just to a simmer and pour over the top. Cook for about 45 minutes.

JP

Pheasants' Breasts and Haggis

In 1996 I published a serious book on the haggis. To help my research, my dear friends the MacSween family, haggis makers *extraordinaire* of Edinburgh, generously loaded me with examples of their art. Now there is, even for me, a limit to the amount of haggis you can eat *au naturel*, so I had to think of other ways to prepare it. I am particularly happy with this dish, because from my pheasant days I know that anything new to do with pheasant is well received. I cooked this recipe for sixty guests at a charity dinner at The Witchery in Edinburgh as a starter and it was a great success. It also works very well as a lunch dish.

1 haggis
1 jar of sweet pickled beets,
drained and chopped
salt and freshly ground pepper
4 pheasant breast halves
(1 per person)
1 packet frozen puff
pastry, thawed
milk or beaten egg to glaze

Remove the haggis from its casing and mix it with the beets. MacSween's haggis is very well flavored, but some are more bland and you may need to add seasoning.

Roll out the puff pastry and cut into squares, each large enough to wrap a pheasant breast. Place a pheasant breast on each square and pile on a layer of the haggis mixture. Fold the pastry over and crimp the edges well to form a package. Brush with milk or beaten egg and bake in a preheated oven at 425°F for 10 minutes. Turn down the heat to 350°F, and continue baking until golden brown, about 20 minutes. Serve with a fruit jelly, or with red-currant sauce made by melting ¾ cup red-currant jelly with 2 tablespoons each of port and lemon juice and seasoning with salt and pepper.

CDW

Buttered Pigeon Breasts

This is the favourite breakfast dish of William Rutherford, the dashing eighteen-year-old son of my friend and colleague Isabel, who refers to them as pigeons' bosoms. Most of us might find this a little too much for breakfast, but it makes an excellent light lunch. Pigeons abound on any working farm, and when they have been shot it is easy just to skin and remove the breasts. Game butchers have them, and farmed pigeons can be found in supermarkets.

2 pigeon breast halves per person
all-purpose flour
salt and freshly ground pepper
paprika
dry mustard powder, such as Coleman's
butter

Roll the pigeon breasts in flour seasoned with salt, pepper, paprika and a pinch of mustard. Fry them gently in melted butter for about 10 minutes, turning occasionally. Serve on toast.

CDW

Confit Béarnaise

In the markets of France, in winter, you will see ready-boned geese and ducks, which are prepared for *confit*. We are not so lucky and have to bone the birds ourselves or find a friendly butcher to do it (another reason to eschew supermarkets, as they won't do this for you).

My dear friend Sir John Scot of Beauclerk often shames me in my idleness. Last winter he killed and turned into *confit* six geese that his son had raised. He gave me a jar of his *confit*, which I treat like gold and which reminds me of the glory of goose fat. Potatoes are never so good as when cooked in goose fat, and you can save it to use again and again.

1 goose, boned, all fat reserved
coarse sea salt
1 teaspoon thyme
1 bay leaf, crushed
½ teaspoon crushed black pepper
½ teaspoon crushed cloves
pure pork fat if needed

TO SERVE:
garlic cloves
chopped potatoes
salt and freshly ground pepper

Cut the goose into 4 pieces, and rub them well with coarse sea salt to which you have added the thyme, bay leaf, black pepper and cloves. Refrigerate for 24 hours.

The next day, wipe the pieces over with paper towels. Remove as much of the fat as possible without damaging the meat, and melt the fat slowly in a heavy pan (cast iron is best). Add the pieces of goose. If the fat does not cover them add some pure pork fat. Simmer very gently for 2–2½ hours or until the meat is cooked and tender. Remove the pieces of goose to sterilized jars. Allow the fat to cook for a further 10–15 minutes, then strain over the goose. Ensure there is at least 2 inches of fat covering the pieces of meat. Leave to cool completely, then cover with aluminum foil and store the *confit* in a cool place.

Here is one good way of using your *confit*. Remove as many pieces of goose as you need, and cut into manageable pieces. In a heavy pan heat the goose fat and gently fry some garlic cloves, then fry some chopped potatoes until they begin to crisp. Add the goose, season with salt and pepper, and allow to heat through. Serve with a green salad.

CDW

Haggis Waldorf

I dreamt this up for a demonstration I did at "Scotland's Larder", at the East Neuk of Fife, for Christopher Trotter. He didn't bat an eyelid when I arrived straight off the plane and told him I had only cooked this recipe in my head. I told the audience too, and they gave me a lot of moral support. It worked very well.

1 head of celery
6 tart apples
4 tablespoons (½ stick) butter
salt and freshly ground pepper
1 haggis, sliced into 8 pieces
grainy mustard
Scotch whisky
heavy cream
red wine vinegar

Wash the celery and cut into julienne strips. Arrange on a serving dish. Peel, core and slice the apples. Melt the butter in a heavy pan and gently soften the apple slices, turning to cook both sides. Season with salt and pepper whilst cooking. Place the apples on top of the celery strips.

Spread one side of each slice of haggis with grainy mustard. Place the slices in the pan, mustard side down, spread the other side with mustard and turn over. Heat through, then place on top of the apple. Deglaze the pan with whisky, which you ignite once it is hot. Add a few spoonfuls of heavy cream and a dash of red wine vinegar, season with salt and pepper, and pour the sauce over the haggis. Serve.

CDW

Warm Chicken Liver Salad

I think warm salads are extremely good. The hot sauce gives a great taste to the salad leaves, one of which should be arugula. Arugula's name derives from the Latin word *eruca* which means caterpillar and which was applied to the plant because of its hairy stem. Fancy! Make sure your salad leaves are fresh and crisp.

½ pound chicken livers
1¼ cups white wine
10 peppercorns
1 garlic clove, peeled and crushed
1 bay leaf
mixed salad leaves
1 tablespoon olive oil
4 tablespoons balsamic vinegar
3 tablespoons heavy cream

Pat the chicken livers dry and cut away any discolored or stringy bits. Marinate the livers overnight in a mixture of the white wine, peppercorns, crushed garlic and bay leaf.

Wash the salad leaves and divide among four plates. Dry the chicken livers (reserve the marinade) and cut into bite-size pieces. Heat the olive oil and fry the chicken livers for about 3 minutes, turning occasionally. Remove the livers from the pan and keep warm. Add the balsamic vinegar to the pan and boil, stirring, until the vinegar is reduced by half. Add 3 tablespoons of the marinade liquid and cook for another minute or two. Remove the pan from the heat and stir in the cream. Arrange the livers on the salad leaves and pour the sauce over.

JP

Stuffed Tomatoes

This is a very good way of stuffing tomatoes, but do try and get some with a really good flavor — difficult but possible.

8 large tomatoes
½ pound ground meat (pork or veal)
½ tablespoon butter
2 cups coarse dry breadcrumbs
1–2 eggs, beaten
3 tablespoons chopped parsley
1 garlic clove, chopped
freshly grated nutmeg
salt and freshly ground pepper
oil

Cut the top off each tomato, scoop the pulp and seeds out and turn the tomatoes upside down on paper towels in order to get rid of all excess liquid. Leave to drain for half an hour.

Fry the meat with the butter in a frying pan until the meat is browned and crumbly. Remove from the heat. Add the toast crumbs, beaten eggs, parsley, garlic, and nutmeg, salt and pepper to taste.

Stuff the tomatoes with the meat mixture and put the tomato lids back on each tomato. Place the tomatoes in a deep ovenproof dish and put a drop of oil on each lid. Bake in a preheated oven at 350°F for 30 minutes.

JP

Paella Verdura

We always think of paella as a fragrant mountain of rice, redolent of saffron, steaming with chicken, pork and shellfish. But there are as many paellas as there are seasons in the year. Here is one for an early summer's day, but you can always improvise and add whatever delights you happen to have in your vegetable garden.

4 tablespoons olive oil
1 onion, chopped
2 garlic cloves, crushed
4 tablespoons chopped parsley
2½ cups Spanish paella rice or use Italian risotto rice
4 cups chicken stock
⅔ cup dry white wine
1 cup each asparagus tips, green beans and baby fava beans in their pods, all cut small
2 Swiss chard leaves, deveined and chopped
2 tomatoes, peeled, seeded and diced
4 fresh anchovy fillets
salt and freshly ground pepper

Heat the oil in a heavy paella pan and fry the onion gently until soft. Add the garlic, half the parsley and the rice, and stir about in the oil. Mix together the stock and wine, add a third to the rice and bring to simmering point. Add the asparagus and chard.

When the stock has been absorbed, add another third plus the green beans, fava beans with their pods and the tomatoes. Stir. When the second batch of stock has been absorbed, add the remainder together with the anchovies. Simmer until all the liquid has been absorbed and the rice is tender (the entire cooking time from first adding the stock is 20–25 minutes). Stir in the rest of the parsley and season to taste.

CDW

Onion Tartlets with Anchovies

These are scrumptious little tarts. Eat while still hot, when they just melt in the mouth.

Makes 20–24

4 tablespoons (½ stick) butter
2 large onions, thinly sliced
6 ounces refrigerated ready-
made pie crust
2 eggs
⅔ cup heavy cream
salt and freshly ground pepper
a little freshly grated nutmeg
20-24 canned anchovy fillets

Melt the butter in a saucepan or frying pan and add the onions. Cover and cook over a low heat until the onions are soft and translucent, stirring occasionally to make sure they don't stick and brown. This will take about 30 minutes.

Meanwhile, roll out the pastry and line 2¼-inch greased tartlet pans. Beat the eggs and cream together and season generously with the salt, pepper and nutmeg. Add the onions and mix well, then divide the mixture among the tartlet pans. Bake in a preheated oven at 375°F for 25–30 minutes. Five minutes before they are ready split the anchovy fillets in half lengthwise and place the two halves in a cross on top of each of the tartlets.

JP

Cheese Soufflé with a Leek Sauce

Do not be afraid of making a soufflé, because they are dead easy. Just refrain from taking a peep while it is cooking.

2 tablespoons (¼ stick) butter
¼ cup all-purpose flour
3 cups milk
3 eggs, separated
¼ cup grated Cheddar cheese
½ teaspoon dry mustard powder
salt and freshly ground pepper

FOR THE LEEK SAUCE:
2 medium leeks, finely chopped with enough of the green part to give an attractive color
1 tablespoon butter
⅔ cup cream

In a saucepan, melt the butter. Stir in the flour and gradually add the milk. Bring to the boil, stirring until you get a smooth sauce. Cool slightly, then add the egg yolks one by one, beating well. Add the cheese, dry mustard powder, salt and pepper. Whisk the egg whites until stiff, and fold gently into the cheese mixture.

Spoon into a 1-quart buttered soufflé dish. Bake in a preheated oven at 375°F for about 30 minutes.

Meanwhile, make the leek sauce. Cook the leeks gently in butter until soft, then purée in a blender or food processor. Add the cream and season to taste. Heat through, and serve with the cheese soufflé.

JP

31

Old Man's Mess

This is a traditional Swedish dish and is normally served as part of a smorgasbord table. It is a speciality of my dear friend, the photographer Carin Simon, who has broken so many men's hearts over the years that I have used the English translation of its name.

1 medium onion, chopped
4 tablespoons (½ stick) butter
1 small can anchovies, drained
4 hard-cooked eggs, chopped

Fry the onion in the butter until golden brown. Add the anchovies and stir them until they fall to bits. Add the eggs, stir well and heat through gently. Serve with toast.

CDW

Eggs Merry Boys

This is a receipt that I came across in the 1960s – Lord knows who the merry boys were. It requires chicken liver pâté as one of its main ingredients, so you'll get two receipts for the price of one. Very good and very rich. There will be more pâté than you need for four servings, so pack the rest into ramekins and keep in the refrigerator to enjoy with hot toast.

FOR THE DUXELLES OF MUSHROOMS:

1½ cups mushrooms
1 small onion, finely chopped
2 shallots, finely chopped
1 tablespoon (⅛ stick) butter
2 teaspoons oil
1 teaspoon finely chopped parsley
pinch of nutmeg
salt and pepper

FOR THE CHICKEN LIVER PÂTÉ:

¾ cup (1½ sticks) butter
1 large onion, chopped
2 garlic cloves, chopped
1 pound chicken livers
½ teaspoon salt
½ teaspoon black pepper
1 teaspoon chopped fresh sage
½ teaspoon chopped fresh thyme
a swig of brandy
2 tablespoons finely chopped parsley

4 eggs
4 tablespoons cream
bread crumbs
freshly grated Parmesan cheese

To make the *duxelles*, wash and finely chop the mushrooms, then squeeze tightly in a cloth to extract as much moisture as possible. Cook the onion and shallots in the butter and oil over a medium heat until lightly browned, then add the mushrooms, parsley, nutmeg, salt and pepper and cook over a fairly high heat so that any moisture left in the mushrooms will evaporate. Leave the mixture to get cold before storing in the refrigerator in a covered jar.

To make the pâté, melt the butter in a saucepan, add the onion and garlic, and cook until the onion is translucent. Trim off any discolored bits from the livers and season with the salt, pepper, sage and thyme. Cook until the livers are firm but still pink inside. Add the brandy and cook for a minute longer. Remove from the heat and add the parsley. Purée the mixture in a blender or food processor.

Butter four ramekin dishes. Put a thin layer of chicken liver pâté on the bottom and cover with the *duxelles* of mushrooms. Break a fresh egg into each ramekin and cover with a spoonful of cream. Place the ramekins in a bain-marie of boiling water and bake in a preheated oven at 450°F for 7–8 minutes. Add a light dusting of bread crumbs and Parmesan and pass briefly under a preheated broiler to brown the crumbs.

JP

Amish Onion Cake

How strange it must be to be Amish, living the life of a farmer of the 1830s amidst that modernised version of the Roman Empire that is present-day America. One can see the German origins of the Amish in this onion cake with its sour cream and poppy seeds.

Serves 4–6

3–4 medium onions, chopped
2 cups (4 sticks) unsalted butter
1 tablespoon poppy seeds
1½ teaspoons each paprika, salt and freshly ground pepper
4 cups all-purpose flour
½ cup cornstarch
1 tablespoon granulated sugar
1 tablespoon baking powder
5 eggs
¾ cup milk
¾ cup sour cream
1 tablespoon dark brown sugar, packed

Cook the onions gently in ½ cup (1 stick) of the butter for about 10 minutes. Stir in the poppy seeds, paprika, salt and pepper and continue to cook until the onions are golden brown. Set aside.

Mix together the flour and cornstarch, granulated sugar and baking powder in a bowl. Add 1¼ cups (2½ sticks) of the remaining butter and rub in to make soft crumbs (this can be done in a food processor). Add 3 of the eggs, one at a time, mixing in well, then add the milk to form a sticky dough.

Beat the last 2 eggs with the remaining ¼ cup (½ stick) butter. Whip in the sour cream and the brown sugar.

Grease a 10-inch round cake pan. Spread the dough in the pan. Cover with the onion mixture and the sour cream mixture. Bake in a preheated oven at 350°F oven for 20–25 minutes. Cool slightly, and serve in wedges.

CDW

Boston Baked Beans

Long before the Plymouth Rock landed on the Pilgrim fathers (or was it the other way round?), the staple diet of the English was the baked bean. That stalwart of middle America, *The Joy of Cooking*, in a burst of what might be anti-British sentiment, says that baked beans are as common in Sweden as they are in the USA. This came as something of a surprise to my Swedish friends. Indeed, Sophie Dow, a well-known Swedish food writer, commented that *"Bruna-bonor-och flask"* (brown beans with pork) was commonly used as a threat to control badly behaved children. Like it or not America, the baked bean is another legacy from us British.

There is an eighteenth-century rhyme about the diet of the English working man that runs: "If you cannot give him bacon – you need not give him beans." Before the potato inveigled its way into our hearts we all ate beans. They were the favorite food of Elizabeth I, who insisted on the addition of winter savory to the dish to kill the flatulent effects.

2 cups dry navy or great northern beans
a 4-ounce piece of salt pork
2–3 tablespoons tomato catsup
1 teaspoon salt
½ teaspoon vinegar
1 onion, chopped
2 tablespoons blackstrap molasses
1 tablespoon dry mustard powder
1 cup beer

Soak the beans overnight in water to cover by several inches. Drain and cover with fresh water. Bring to the boil and simmer gently for 1½ hours or until tender. Drain the beans (reserve the water) and place in a greased ovenproof dish. Add all the other ingredients. Cover and bake in a preheated oven at 250°F for 7–9 hours. Add some of the reserved bean water if they appear to be drying out. Cook uncovered for the last hour.

CDW

MAIN COURSES

Jennifer uses her charms on embassy chauffeur Joseph Gouveia – or is he just interested in the motorcycle?

CLARISSA WRITES: It always seems to me that the hardest course to get right in a dinner party is the main course. I can always think of dozens of appetizers, even ones you can make the day before. Puddings (desserts), which I can find a chore to make, present themselves as ideas quite easily. But the balance, the core of the meal with its accompaniments of vegetables and sauces, is what sorts out the cook from the microwave.

Coordination, the getting of the main course on to the table at the right time, at the right temperature and with all the right bits is not really difficult, it just requires a bit of thought and even some helpful notes to aid your timing. Do not try to run before you can walk: often, keeping it sim-

ple and taking the trouble to shop for the best ingredients is the wisest course. Do allow time for your guests to enjoy their pre-dinner drinks and to eat their appetizers, but do not fall into the trap, if someone arrives really late, of further postponing the meal to allow them to have a drink.

For the program, we cooked a regimental dinner for the Gurkhas. The Army is reluctant to put forward this image, but one of the finest training grounds for chefs seeking a wide repertoire is the Army Catering Corps. I for one would be happy to see more chefs trained with the ACC's "use your brains" attitude, rather than the learning by rote which prevails at so many culinary schools nowadays.

Jennifer regrets that the size of her flat prevents her from having large dinner parties at present, but in her time she has hosted some corkers. I like to think of her cooking for her dashing Hussars in Benghazi on merely a Baby Belling, the saucepans piled high on top of each other and the Shikor roasting within, to be served with lashings of bread sauce.

I love dinner parties; to me they are the happiest moments of my cookery life. A beautifully-laid table with fine glasses, silver and linen, and the company of your friends enjoying your efforts, is what it is all about. It is always tragic when you go to someone's house for dinner and the food lets the occasion down. Keep it simple and do what you can, do not try out any experiments on a dinner party. I hope that this selection of main courses will make your dinners run more smoothly.

TOP *Clarissa practises what she preaches, shopping for the best ingredients*

LEFT *Yes, it was the motorcycle after all! Mr Gouveia goes for a ride*

Robert May's Salmon

The phenomenon of celebrity chefs writing books is not new: the advent of the Stuarts in 1603 had a very sophisticating effect on English food, and court-trained chefs were the Emeril Lagasse of their day. Robert May, who was one of the finest of these, begins his book by apologising to his fellow chefs for giving away trade secrets, a nicety that is missing today. This recipe continues my search for interesting things to do with salmon. I cooked it for an article in the *Daily Express* on the Sotheby's auction of cookery books, and it was deemed delicious.

a 2-pound *darne* of salmon (thick slice cut across the fish, just behind the head)
3 oranges, peeled and sliced
2 teaspoons freshly grated nutmeg
salt
½ cup red wine
juice of 1 orange

Skin the *darne* of salmon. In a sauté pan, or other pan just large enough to accommodate the fish, make a layer of orange slices. Put the salmon on top and season with the nutmeg and salt. Pack the remaining orange slices around the sides and over the top. Pour on the wine and orange juice and bring to the boil. Cover and simmer for 15 minutes or until the salmon is just cooked. Serve with sippets (triangles) of toasted bread – made from good bread, not sliced or supermarket.

CDW

A Lobster for Lady Strathmore

As the result of a rather jolly meeting in a bread shop, Jennifer and I went to Glamis to demonstrate. Isobel, the present Countess, had decided that pineapples were a better bet than flowers in mid-winter Scotland and the whole house was decorated with them. Glamis is a splendid castle, and she and her husband were splendid hosts, so I thought I would invent a splendid dish in remembrance of the occasion, using pineapple halves for a smashing presentation. The dish is lovely spooned over rice.

2 live lobsters (about 1½ pounds each)
1 large pineapple
4 tablespoons (½ stick) unsalted butter
2 shallots, finely chopped
1¼ cups heavy cream
salt and freshly ground pepper
5 tablespoons capers
2 sun-dried tomatoes

Cook the lobsters using your approved method. I put mine into lukewarm water, bring to the boil and cook for 10 minutes to each 1 pound. Remove the lobster meat from the shells and cut into 1-inch chunks.

Cut the pineapple in half from top to bottom and scoop out the flesh, hollowing out the shell halves but leaving them intact. Squeeze the juice from the flesh, then discard the flesh.

Melt half of the butter in a saucepan and gently fry the shallots until they just color. Add the cream, bring to the boil and reduce by one third. Add the lobster meat and half the pineapple juice, season and bring back to the boil. Stir in the capers and tomatoes. Divide the mixture between the two pineapple halves. Dot with the remaining butter, and put under a preheated broiler for 5 minutes or until the surface is golden. Each half serves 2 people.

CDW

Turbot Kabobs with Tomato and Cumin Sauce

Turbot is very expensive and a great treat, one of the noblest of fish. Alternatively, you could use another firm fish for these kabobs, such as halibut, monkfish or even the humble rockfish or pollack.

1½–2 pounds turbot, skinned and filleted
2 tablespoons olive oil
juice of half a lemon
salt and freshly ground pepper

FOR THE SAUCE:
1 large onion, chopped
1 garlic clove, chopped
2 tablespoons (¼ stick) unsalted butter
1 tablespoon olive oil
14-ounce can plum tomatoes, drained
1 teaspoon chile powder
1 teaspoon ground cumin
1 tablespoon honey
salt and freshly ground pepper
⅔ cup heavy cream

fresh bay leaves

Cut the turbot into 1–1½-inch cubes. Mix together the olive oil, lemon juice, salt and pepper and pour over the fish. Cover and leave to marinate for half an hour.

To make the sauce, fry the chopped onion and garlic in the butter and olive oil gently until the onion is translucent. Add the drained tomatoes, chile powder and cumin. Stir, then leave to simmer for 45 minutes, stirring occasionally. Purée in a blender or food processor. Add the honey and season with salt and pepper. Allow to cool. Add the cream and warm through for serving, but do not allow to boil.

Thread the cubes of fish and bay leaves alternately on to skewers. Cook under a preheated broiler, turning occasionally. Serve with the tomato and cumin sauce.

JP

Turbot with Watercress and Pickled Walnuts

I make people down south tired with my endless praise for the wonderful fish in my beloved Scotland, and more especially for my joy in the friendship of my dear Mr Clarke who dispenses such delights in Fisherrow, Musselburgh. Turbot is a great fish. People complain that it is too expensive, but it is so firm and meaty that you don't need as much of it as less satisfying fish. You can do this dish with a 2-pound small whole turbot, but it is more usual to make it with one 6-ounce steak per person.

4 turbot steaks (6 ounces each per person)
½ cup onions, sliced
about 2 cups mixed white wine and fish stock
12 pickled walnuts (available at specialty stores), plus extra to garnish
4 tablespoons (½ stick) butter
a bunch of watercress, finely chopped
salt and freshly ground pepper

Put the turbot steaks in a pan with the onions and enough wine and stock to cover. Bring to the boil, then poach gently for 15 minutes. Remove the fish to a serving dish and keep warm. Strain the liquid and reserve.

Mash the pickled walnuts. Combine them with the butter, 1¼ cups of the fish cooking liquid and the chopped watercress. Season. Bring to the boil and simmer for a few minutes. Pour this sauce over the fish, garnish with pickled walnut halves and serve.

CDW

Note: if you can't get turbot, flounder fillets or pompano could be used instead.

Brisket of Beef with Onion Sauce

Get your brisket from a good butcher. It should be marbled throughout with fat, not a nasty little knob of meat as is found in supermarkets.

3-pound brisket of beef
salt
1 large onion, cut into quarters
a couple of parsley and thyme sprigs
2 carrots, cut into chunks
2 bay leaves
1 small turnip, cut into chunks
12 peppercorns

FOR THE ONION SAUCE:
1 pound onions, chopped
6 tablespoons (¾ stick) butter
⅔ cup flour
⅔ cup milk
ground mace
freshly grated nutmeg
salt and freshly ground pepper

Place the brisket in a large, heavy pan with all the other ingredients and cover with water. Bring to the boil, then lower the heat and simmer gently for 2½–3 hours.

Towards the end of the brisket cooking time, make the sauce. Cook the onions gently in 4 tablespoons of the butter until they are translucent; set aside to cool. Melt the remaining butter in a saucepan and stir in the flour. Gradually add 2 cups of the brisket cooking liquid and milk, stirring all the time. Place over a medium-high heat and bring to the boil. Add a pinch each of mace and nutmeg. Turn down the heat and simmer the sauce for 2–3 minutes, stirring occasionally. Pureé the cooked onions and add to the sauce. Season well. Set aside until ready to reheat for serving.

Remove the brisket from the pan and strain the stock, discarding vegetables and herbs. Replace the brisket and remaining stock in the pan and bring back to the boil. Turn down the heat so that the stock is gently simmering. You can now add the vegetables you wish to serve with the brisket such as raw chunks of carrot and turnip or the white part of a couple of leeks. When adding the vegetables bear in mind the length of time each one takes to cook, so that they are all ready at the same time.

Remove the brisket from the stock and place on a large serving dish surrounded by the vegetables. Serve with the onion sauce.

JP

Royal Brisket

The second half of the eighteenth century was the great age of the political taverner, a patron who offered good food and comfortable surroundings in which his well-to-do customers could meet and discuss the political changes in America or France without risking legal charges. This recipe, published in 1783, is from one such taverner, or "celebrity chef": John Farley of the London Tavern. I find the recipe particularly interesting because of the use of oysters – reminiscent of that great Australian dish, carpetbag steak (note the date). Brisket is a neglected cut of beef, but as no doubt by now you will be frequenting a proper butcher, obtaining a brisket should not be a problem.

a 2-pound boned, rolled brisket of beef
4 ounces bacon, chopped
4 fresh oysters, chopped
2 tablespoons chopped parsley
freshly grated nutmeg
salt and freshly ground pepper
½ cup all-purpose flour
4 tablespoons (½ stick) butter
2½ cups red wine
2 cups beef stock

Make slits 1-inch apart all over the roast. Insert the bacon, oysters and parsley alternately into the slits. Season the roast with nutmeg, salt and pepper and dredge with the flour. Brown the meat in the butter. Put into a large casserole with the wine and stock and bring to the boil. Cover tightly and cook in a preheated oven at 350°F for 3 hours.

Remove the roast to a dish and keep warm. Boil the cooking liquid to reduce it, stirring to mix in the sediments in the bottom of the casserole, and pour over the meat. Serve with sweet pickles and fresh crisp vegetables. (Notice the word "crisp" – this was in use before the dreaded Mrs Beeton.)

CDW

Beef with Chestnuts, Pears, and Almonds

When the redoubtable Carlos and Isabella (see page 147) retired we had a whole wave of Catalan servants, all of whom seemed to be named in pairs. We had Secundo and Secunda, Seraphim and Sarafina, Hermanios and Harmonia (I promise you this is true). Whether or not these were names chosen by the employment agency in the tradition of Edwardian parlor maids I don't know, but they seemed quite happy with them. The Catalans are splendid cooks and love using peanuts in the medieval fashion. This recipe is for a sauce to be served with beef, whether in a piece or as a steak. I like to serve it with a good short rib roasted for 17 minutes to each 1 pound: start in a hot oven, 450°F, and reduce to 325°F after 20 minutes.

2 tablespoons olive oil
3 tomatoes, peeled, seeded and chopped
1 garlic clove
1 slice stale bread
1¼ cups ground almonds
1¼ cups dry white wine
8 ounces chestnuts, peeled and chopped
3 pears, poached in red wine until tender

Heat the oil in a heavy pan and fry the tomatoes until soft. Grind together the garlic and bread in a mortar and pestle, and add to the tomatoes together with the ground almonds. Pour in the white wine, stir and reduce to the consistency of thick gravy. Add the chestnuts. Core and roughly chop the pears, add to the pan and heat through. Serve with the beef.

CDW

Loin of Pork Stuffed with Cèpes or Truffles

This is a wonderful dish to be eaten either hot or cold. In Périgord it is made with black truffles, and if you happen to have a small jar they are the ideal. Otherwise a very good flavor is achieved by using the Italian dried cèpes, or *funghi porcini secchi*. What is most important is that the pork should be first class, from a proper butcher who deals with well-bred pigs.

a 4-pound loin of pork
salt and freshly ground pepper
3 truffles or about 2 ounces dried cèpes (porcini)
garlic cloves, thinly sliced
2 cups hot meat stock or water
⅔ cup dry white wine

Ask your butcher to bone the loin, but keep the bones for the cooking. If you are using dried cèpes, cover them with warm water and leave to soak for 30 minutes or so until they are soft. Drain, reserving the liquid. Lay the meat on a board and season well with salt and pepper. Cut the truffles or cèpes into little pieces and lay at intervals along the meat interspersed with slivers of garlic. Roll the meat up and tie it with string into a long bolster shape. Place it in a roasting pan surrounded by the bones and the skin cut into strips. Roast in a preheated oven at 325°F for 30 minutes. Pour in the hot stock or water, the wine and the liquid from soaking the cèpes. Cover the pan and cook for a further 2–2½ hours.

Remove the pork and keep hot. Strain the juices and reduce, then season to taste. Serve with the sliced pork. Or, if serving the pork cold, pour off the juices into a bowl and chill. Remove the fat, but keep it for frying bread or little potatoes — it has a splendid flavor. The juices will have jellied and should be chopped and arranged around the cold pork in a serving dish. Serve with what you will, such as a fine salad and some sautéed potatoes.

JP

Oxford John

This is an excellent dish if you want the taste of leg of lamb or mutton, but for reasons of expense, quantity or time you don't want to buy the whole roast. In Scotland this particular cut has the splendid name "giget chops".

½ teaspoon each ground mace, dried thyme and chopped parsley
½ cup onion, finely chopped
4 slices of lamb or mutton, cut from the leg (4 ounces each)
4 tablespoons (½ stick) butter
¼ cup all-purpose flour
2 cups lamb stock
juice of 1 lemon
salt and freshly ground pepper

Mix together the mace, thyme, parsley and onion, and coat the lamb slices on both sides with this. Gently fry the meat in the butter for 10 minutes, turning once. Remove the meat and set aside. Stir the flour into the fat in the pan, add the stock and simmer for 5 minutes, stirring. Return the meat to the pan and add the lemon juice. Simmer for a further 5 minutes. Adjust seasoning and serve.

CDW

Lamb Couscous

A fine festive dish to set in the middle of a well-crowded table. They present the whole sheep on a vast tray in the Middle East, eyes and all. Yum yum.

2 tablespoons olive oil
2 medium onions, cut into thick slices
1 large garlic clove, finely chopped
1½ teaspoons ground cilantro
1½ teaspoons ground cumin
1 teaspoon ground cinnamon, plus extra for sprinkling
½ teaspoon saffron strands
½ teaspoon ground ginger
1 tablespoon tomato paste
2-pound boneless leg of lamb, cubed
½ teaspoon harissa
salt and freshly ground pepper
½ cup dry garbanzo beans, soaked overnight, or use ½ can (adjust amount to to personal taste — I love garbanzo beans)
2 large carrots, cut into chunks
2 small turnips, quartered
1 eggplant, cut into chunks
3 zucchini, cut into chunks
⅓ cup raisins
2 tomatoes, quartered
a large handful of parsley, chopped
1 large handful of fresh cilantro, chopped
1 pound (2½ cups) couscous

Heat the oil in a large saucepan, add the onions and cook for a few minutes to soften. Add the garlic, all the spices and the tomato paste and cook together for a few minutes, stirring. Add the cubed lamb and enough water (or stock if you have it) just to cover the lamb. Stir in ½ teaspoon of harissa (you can add more later on if you find it is not hot enough for you) and season with salt and pepper. Add the soaked dry garbanzo beans (wait if using canned). Bring to the boil, then simmer gently for about 30 minutes. Add the carrots and turnips, and cook for another 30 minutes before adding the eggplant, zucchini, raisins and canned garbanzo beans. After a further 20 minutes add the tomatoes and about half of the parsley and fresh cilantro, keeping the remainder for the garnish. Check the seasoning and leave to cook for a further 5 minutes.

Meanwhile, prepare the couscous according to the package instructions.

To serve, pile the couscous on a large serving dish and sprinkle with a little extra cinnamon. Arrange the meat and vegetables in the center of the couscous, and sprinkle with the rest of the parsley and fresh cilantro. Serve the broth in a separate bowl with smaller bowls for each person so that they can ladle out their own broth as a sauce, to which they can add extra harissa to their taste.

JP

Illustrated overleaf

Sabra Chicken

A sabra is a native-born Israeli. This recipe comes from Oded Schwartz's brilliant book *In Search of Plenty*, soon to be reprinted in the UK by Kyle Cathie.

½ cup dry white wine
½ cup fresh orange juice
zest of ½ orange, grated or julienned
salt and freshly ground pepper
paprika
a small chicken, cut into 8 pieces
4 tablespoons olive oil
1 onion, finely chopped
8 olives, pitted and blanched to remove excess salt
chopped fresh mint to garnish

Mix together the wine, orange juice and orange zest with a seasoning of salt, pepper and paprika. Add the chicken and marinate for 2 hours.

Heat the oil in a large, heavy pan. Remove the chicken from the marinade and dry well with paper towels, then brown well on all sides in the oil. Remove from the pan and keep warm. Add the onions to the oil remaining in the pan and cook until they change color. Add the marinade and simmer for 10 minutes. Return the chicken to the pan and simmer gently over a low heat for 35–40 minutes or until cooked.

Lift out the chicken pieces, cover and keep hot. Add the olives to the liquid and boil rapidly until it starts to thicken. Pour over the chicken. Sprinkle with chopped mint and serve.

CDW

Hot and Spicy Chicken with a Yellow Pepper Sauce

Do not overcook the chicken breast halves, or they will be dry and taste like blotting paper.

1 tablespoon ground cumin
¼ teaspoon chile powder
salt and freshly ground pepper
4 boneless chicken
breast halves
olive oil

FOR THE PEPPER SAUCE:
1 medium onion, finely
chopped
olive oil
1 garlic clove, finely chopped
¼ teaspoon chile powder
½ teaspoon ground cumin
⅔ cup dry white wine
6 tablespoons red
wine vinegar
3 large yellow bell peppers,
broiled or roasted, then
skinned and cored
1¼ cups chicken stock
lemon juice

Mix together the cumin, chile powder, salt and pepper, and rub the chicken breast halves with the mixture. Sauté the chicken breast halves in olive oil over medium heat for about 10 minutes or until cooked through, turning from time to time.

Meanwhile, for the sauce, sauté the onion in a little olive oil until softened. Add the garlic, chile powder and cumin and cook for a few more minutes. Add the wine and vinegar and bring to the boil, then simmer until the liquid is reduced to about 2 tablespoons. Purée the bell peppers with the chicken stock in a blender or food processor. Add to the reduced liquid with a good squeeze of lemon juice, and adjust the seasoning. Heat through before serving with the chicken.

JP

Lemon and Saffron Chicken

Saffron is one of the most expensive spices there is, but you need very little and the flavor it produces is well worth the price.

a good pinch of saffron threads

2 tablespoons hot water

1 medium-sized chicken, cut up (preferably free-range)

4 tablespoons (½ stick) butter

1 tablespoon oil

1 onion, sliced

1 large carrot, cut into finger-length chunks

3 celery stalks, sliced

1¼ cups good chicken stock

juice of half a lemon

3 fl oz white wine

salt and freshly ground pepper

FOR THE SAUCE:

3 tablespoons (⅜ stick) butter

6 tablespoons all-purpose flour

2 egg yolks

⅔ cup heavy cream

grated zest of 1 lemon

1¼ cups sliced mushrooms, sautéed in butter

fresh cilantro, chopped

salt and freshly ground pepper

lemon juice (optional)

Fry the saffron threads in a dry frying pan for a few minutes, then soak in the hot water for 15 minutes. Melt the butter with the oil in the frying pan and fry the chicken pieces until they change color. Lay the chicken pieces on top of the sliced onions, carrots and celery in a casserole dish. Add the chicken stock, lemon juice, a generous dash of white wine and the saffron liquid, and season with salt and pepper. Cook in a preheated oven at 400°F for 1¼–1½ hours. Remove the chicken pieces, carrots and celery and keep warm. Strain the cooking liquid into a saucepan. Add the white wine and boil rapidly for a few minutes to reduce to 2 cups. Reserve for the sauce

To make the sauce, melt the butter in a saucepan, add the flour and blend with the butter. Slowly add the reserved cooking liquid and cook, stirring constantly, over a low heat until it comes to the boil. Simmer sauce gently, stirring occasionally, for 5–10 minutes.

Beat egg yolks, cream and lemon zest together.

Remove the sauce from heat and stir in the egg mixture. Season with salt and pepper and add mushrooms and chopped fresh cilantro to taste. Add a little lemon juice if necessary.

JP

Steamroller Chicken

This is a Peshwari dish, so named because the chickens are butterflied and flattened to look as if they have been run over by a steamroller.

2 small chickens
4 tablespoons ghee (clarified butter)

FOR THE PASTE:
1 onion, chopped
a 1-inch piece of fresh ginger, chopped
3 tablespoons ghee
1 tablespoon ground cilantro
1½ teaspoon ground cumin
1 teaspoon turmeric
1 teaspoon cayenne pepper
½ teaspoon ground cardamom
¼ teaspoon ground cloves
¼ teaspoon ground cinnamon
2 garlic cloves, smashed
juice of 1 lemon

Combine all the ingredients for the paste in a food processor, and process to a fine texture. Halve the chickens by cutting down the center of the backbone and whack them hard with the flat of a cleaver until they are flattened. Rub the chickens all over with the paste and put in a bowl with the remainder of the paste. Cover and leave in the fridge overnight.

Broil the chickens under a preheated broiler for 10 minutes on each side, basting with both the marinade and the ghee. Serve with naan bread and chutneys.

CDW

Coq au Vin

Do not be dismayed at the color of this sauce, which is rather dingy. It's meant to look like that. If your chicken is not a real free-range bird you can reduce the cooking time. Take care not to overcook, which will result in the meat shredding.

1 bottle of red wine
a few sprigs of fresh thyme
2 bay leaves
a few sprigs of parsley
1 medium-sized chicken, cut up (use free-range for more flavor)
1 tablespoon vegetable oil
4 ounces sliced bacon, cut into strips or lardoons
2 onions, chopped
all-purpose flour
1 glass of brandy
2 garlic cloves, chopped
4 ounces mushrooms, halved or quartered if large
20 pearl onions
4 tablespoons (½ stick) butter
2 teaspoons sugar
beurre manié, made with 1 teaspoon each all-purpose flour and butter mixed to a paste
1 tablespoon chopped parsley

Bring the red wine to the boil with the sprigs of thyme and parsley and the bay leaves, then leave to cool for 1 hour. Pour the wine over the chicken pieces and marinate for 12 hours.

Fry the bacon in a frying pan; remove with a slotted spoon. Add the oil to the pan and fry the onions until softened. Remove the chicken pieces from the marinade and pat dry with kitchen paper. Dust the chicken pieces with a little flour, then put them in the frying pan and brown them lightly. Pour in the warmed brandy and flambé it. Transfer the chicken pieces and liquid to a casserole and add the bacon, strained marinade, garlic and mushrooms. Cover and cook in a preheated oven at 300°F for about 1 hour.

In the meantime, fry the pearl onions in butter with the sugar and a little water until glazed. Add to the casserole and cook for a further 30 minutes. If the sauce needs thickening, stir in a few small bits of beurre manié. Remove the casserole from the oven and sprinkle the chopped parsley over before serving.

JP

Turkey Vendageuse

It seems strange to think of French grape pickers eating turkey, but this recipe, found in a strange old book called *Customs in the Perigord and Quercy*, seems to suggest otherwise. I was not really a fan of turkey until this Christmas, when I ordered a real free-range bird from the Chatsworth farm shop at the advice of my friend, the food expert Henrietta Green. The taste and texture of the turkey was so different that I was converted. However, even with the rather flaccid examples on supermarket shelves, this is a good dish.

Serves 6

6 turkey cutlets,
approximately 5 ounces each
3 garlic cloves, cut into slivers
2 slices of unsmoked bacon,
cut into short, thin strips
1 tablespoon pork, goose or
duck fat
1 onion, sliced
1 carrot, sliced
6 whole cloves
1 bouquet garni
1¼ cups chicken stock
salt and freshly ground pepper
1 tablespoon cognac
6 artichoke hearts, canned or
thawed frozen
1½ cups seedless green grapes

Flatten the turkey cutlets and remove any skin. Make small slits all over the turkey fillets and stick in the slivers of garlic and bacon. Smear the fat over the base of a shallow flameproof casserole, and scatter in the onion and carrot. Put the turkey fillets on top and add the cloves and bouquet garni. Add the stock and season with salt and pepper. Cook in a preheated oven at 350°F for 25 minutes, basting frequently; the turkey fillets should be cooked through but moist and tender.

Transfer the turkey to a hot dish and keep warm. Skim off the excess fat from the cooking liquid in the pan and deglaze with the cognac, stirring well. Add the artichoke hearts and grapes, and reduce the sauce by boiling fiercely for a couple of minutes. Surround the turkey fillets with the artichoke hearts and grapes. Strain the sauce and spoon over the meat.

CDW

B'stilla

Sweetened pastry for savory pies is very common in southern Mediterranean countries. A sugared finish for phyllo goes very well with the spicy contents of this pie.

1 medium-sized chicken, cut up
6 tablespoons (¾ stick) butter, melted
1 large onion, chopped
½ teaspoon ground ginger
½ teaspoon saffron threads
½ teaspoon ground cinnamon, plus extra for sprinkling
½ teaspoon pumpkin pie spice
salt and freshly ground pepper
2 teaspoons semolina
2 tablespoons finely chopped parsley
1 tablespoon finely chopped fresh cilantro
9 sheets of phyllo pastry
2 cups blanched almonds, roughly chopped and sautéed in butter
1 egg yolk, beaten
1 tablespoon confectioners' sugar

Put the chicken pieces in a large saucepan with 2 tablespoons of the butter, the onion, ginger, saffron, cinnamon, mixed spice, salt and pepper. Add enough water to come about half way up the chicken pieces. Bring to the boil, then simmer very gently until the chicken is tender, about 20–25 minutes, adding a little extra water if necessary during cooking.

When the chicken is cooked, drain off the stock and reserve. Skin and bone the chicken and cut the meat into small strips. Return a scant 2 cups of the stock to the saucepan and mix in the semolina until the stock is slightly thickened. Be careful not to add too much semolina or you will end up with a paste. Remove from the heat and add the parsley and cilantro.

Brush a large pie dish or pan (about 2 inches deep) with melted butter. Cover with a sheet of phyllo that has been well brushed with melted butter, placing it buttered side down. Add another 6 sheets of pastry to the dish, brushing each one well with melted butter and placing it on top of the previous sheet at an angle. Sprinkle a few of the chopped almonds between each sheet. The sheets should overhang the side of the pie dish. Mix a little of the stock mixture with the chicken and place in the dish. Add more stock if necessary, so the mixture is nicely moist but not wet. Bring the overhanging pastry over the filling, making sure each sheet has been brushed with butter and adding the remaining almonds between layers. Add two more buttered sheets of phyllo, tucking these sheets down between the sides of the pie and the dish. Paint the top of the pie with the beaten egg yolk. Bake in a preheated oven at 375°F for 45–60 minutes or until golden brown. Serve hot, sprinkled with the confectioners' sugar and extra cinnamon.

JP

Duck on the Yangtze

Back to the Yangtze of my childhood, where I was raised. It must have left its mark as I adore all Chinese food and their spices and sauces. This is not a strictly traditional Chinese recipe, but one I have adapted.

4 large duck breast halves
2 tablespoons gin
2 teaspoons five spice powder
1¼ cups dry white wine
grated zest of ½ orange
juice of 1 orange
1½ tablespoons honey
1½ tablespoons soy sauce
1-inch piece of fresh ginger, shredded

Wipe the duck breast halves and prick the skin all over. Mix 1 tablespoon of gin with 1 teaspoon of five spice powder and brush over the duck breast halves. Roast the duck breast halves in a preheated oven at 425°F for about 30 minutes or until cooked to taste. Brush the duck with the gin and five spice powder mixture two or three times while cooking. Remove the duck breast halves from the pan and keep warm. Pour off excess fat from the pan and put the remaining juices in a small saucepan. Add the white wine, bring to the boil and reduce by half. Add the remaining gin and five spice powder, the orange zest and juice, honey, soy sauce and shredded ginger. Lower the heat and simmer until the liquid is reduced and syrupy, stirring all the time.

Place the duck breast halves on a hot serving dish and spoon the glaze over before serving.

JP

Stuffed Quail with White Wine

I am very fond of eating little birds. They take a long time to eat if you want to get every last morsel out of them, and I like the texture. Quails don't have a lot of flavor, so you can add anything you like to enhance them.

4 quails
salt and freshly ground pepper
4 tablespoons cooked rice
4 dried apricots, chopped
a good pinch of ground ginger
½ teaspoon grated orange zest
1 tablespoon pine nuts
½ cup melted butter
6 tablespoons white wine
juice of ½ orange
cognac

Wipe the quails, and season inside and out with salt and pepper. Combine the rice, chopped apricots, ginger, grated orange zest and pine nuts and moisten with a little melted butter. Stuff the quails with the mixture and place them in a roasting pan. Brush the quails with melted butter. Roast in a preheated oven at 450°F for 10 minutes. Reduce the heat to 300°F and roast for a further 15 minutes, basting frequently with a mixture of the wine (which should be boiled to reduce by about a third), the orange juice and about 4 tablespoons of melted butter. Remove the quails to a serving dish and keep warm. Taste the liquid in the roasting pan and, if necessary, add pepper and salt, then pour the liquid over the quails. Pour warmed cognac over the quails and ignite. Serve at once.

JP

PUDDINGS (DESSERTS)

Fresh fruit makes for good puddings, and the freshest of all is picked from the fields

CLARISSA WRITES: Jennifer does not really like puddings, as desserts are known in the UK; she accepts that they are a neccesity of life and that she must make them for her friends, but she is really happier finishing a meal with some cheese. That does not mean that she does not make some very inspired examples, but it is not a passion of hers.

I, however, live in Scotland, a country with a very sweet tooth. I sometimes think that my guests spend the meal in suspended animation, waiting for the pudding. I have another reason for my fondness for puddings: men love puddings, and I am very fond of men!

The other angle on a good pudding is that, however poor the rest of the meal, if your guests finish with an excellent dessert, they will go away with a better memory of it. I know a restaurant which seems to work on that principle, and which has flourished for years.

I like my puddings to be lavish. Not for me the insipidity of a fruit salad made with tasteless, "nuked" tropical fruit, or some healthy concoction based on yogurt or crème fraîche. A pudding should be unequivocally a pudding. St Honoré, the patron saint of pastry chefs, was not, I feel, a man who dallied with yogurt. But you don't have to take my word for it: at your next dinner party, try serving two puddings, one in my style with cream and meringue and delicious things, and

Another day, another conquest – for the motorcycle.
Sound recordist Rupert Ivey takes charge this time

one soi-disant healthy variety, and see which you are left with to carry back to the kitchen. In fact, it is quite a good idea to have two puddings anyway, as people always feel spoilt by having a choice. Don't think of them as alternatives, though – people will invariably try a bit of both!

In Britain we have a splendid tradition of puddings, which may be due to the fact that however many cooks you employed, the pudding was usually the work of the lady of the house. Preparing a good pudding therefore became a matter of honor, and you know what that can lead to. You can still see this today: go to a smart dinner party and watch the look on the hostess's face as she wheels in the pudding, and you will instantly identify with it. We have all been there, haven't we?

The other good thing about puddings is that one can usually make them in advance so that time is on your side. On an everyday level one may not always have time to make a pudding,

but good, home-grown fruit in summer or some fruit purée from the freezer in winter – or even better, some bottled fruit if you can manage it – always make an easy dessert. Don't forget ice-cream either. Where I live, in Musselburgh, we have two ice-cream makers. I also recently "designed" an ice-cream for a friend who is a keen maker, and was reminded of just how good home-made ice-cream can be. I am now even thinking of getting a house-cow to supply unpasteurised cream, but I don't know who would keep it for me.

Jennifer enjoys an English summer day while picking
fruit at the Kitchen Garden

Eton Mess

This must be one of the easiest puddings to make. Other suitable fruits, such as raspberries, also look luscious.

1 pound strawberries
⅓ cup sugar
2 teaspoons Kirsch
6 small meringues
2½ cups heavy cream, whipped until thick

Crush the strawberries lightly, and sprinkle with the sugar and Kirsch. Leave in the fridge for 2–3 hours. Crush the meringues coarsely and fold into the strawberries with the whipped cream.

JP

Lemon Posset

Possets were all the rage in the later Middle Ages. They were usually made with hot milk mixed with hot beer, sherry etc. and various spices. Excellent for keeping the cold at bay. This one is far more luxurious — a very old English recipe said to have been favored by Samuel Pepys.

3 sugar cubes
1 lemon
2½ cups heavy cream
⅔ cup dry white wine
2–3 tablespoons sugar
3 large egg whites (preferably free-range eggs)

Rub the sugar cubes over the rind of the lemon to absorb as much oil as possible from the zest. Crush the sugar cubes in a large bowl and add the cream. Start whisking, gradually adding the white wine and the juice of the lemon. Stir in the sugar. Beat the egg whites until stiff, and carefully fold into the cream mixture. Spoon into individual glasses and serve, decorated with a tiny piece of sugar-coated lemon zest and some crisp cookies.

JP

Chocolate, Orange, and Hazelnut Mousse

"A hunter called Nathanial Welk went out one day to shoot an elk. A random shot discharged too loose brought down a lovely chocolate mousse." That is what we used to chant when we were young. It is always handy to have the odd chocolate mousse around, and this is an unusual one.

½ cup hazelnuts
¾ cup chunky orange marmalade
1 tablespoon rum
24 ladyfingers
6 tablespoons (¾ stick) unsalted butter, at room temperature
¼ cup sugar
14 ounces bittersweet chocolate
2 tablespoons milk
3 eggs, separated, plus 1 extra egg white

Skin the nuts by toasting them on a baking pan in a preheated 425°F oven for 8 minutes, then rubbing the skin off with a dish towel as they cool. Cut the nuts in half. Heat the marmalade with the rum until it melts, then dip the ladyfingers in this mixture and use them to line the sides of a 10-inch cylindrical mold reserving the remainder.

Cream together the butter and sugar. Melt the chocolate with the milk, and add to the butter mixture. Beat in the egg yolks, one by one, and stir in the nuts. Add the remaining marmalade mixture. Whisk the egg whites until stiff, then fold into the chocolate orange mixture. Pour into the mold. Chill until set. Turn out the mousse to serve.

CDW

Mrs Anne Bearley's Rhubarb Whim Wham

This is from an excellent little book, *The Lincolnshire Cookery Book*, put together and sold for St John's Ambulance, a very worthy cause indeed. And a most delicious pudding it is.

1 pound rhubarb
1 orange
2 tablespoons red-currant jelly
2 glasses of sweet sherry
1 sherry glass of brandy
18 ladyfingers

FOR THE TOPPING:
½ cup unblanched almonds, chopped
2 tablespoons (¼ stick) unsalted butter
1 tablespoon sugar

2 cups heavy cream
1 egg white
1 tablespoon sugar

Cut the rhubarb into small dice. Thinly pare the zest from the orange and cut into fine julienne strips (or make strips with a citrus zester). Place the rhubarb, the juice from the orange, the strips of zest and the gelatin powder in a saucepan and cook gently until the rhubarb is just tender, but still has a little bite. Pour into a dainty dish to cool, then add the sherry and brandy. Break the ladyfingers into quarters and gently mix into the rhubarb.

To make the topping, sauté the almonds in the butter until golden. Add the sugar, mix well and allow to cool.

Just before serving, whip the cream to soft peaks. Whisk the egg white with the sugar until stiff, and fold into the cream. Cover the rhubarb with the cream, then sprinkle all over with the almonds.

JP

St Emilion au Chocolat

An elegant pudding for chocoholics, rich and ravishing.

Serves 8

1 pound macaroons
1 liqueur glass of rum
4 ounces bittersweet chocolate
2 teaspoons water
4 tablespoons (½ stick) butter,
at room temperature
¼ cup sugar
⅔ cup milk
1 egg yolk

Sprinkle the rum over the macaroons. Try to do this evenly as the macaroons should not be too wet.

Place the chocolate and water in a heatproof bowl set over gently simmering water and leave to melt slowly.

Cream the butter with the sugar. Scald the milk and leave to cool slightly (it should still be hot), then beat into the egg yolk. Add the melted chocolate to the butter and sugar mixture, then stir in the milk mixture. Stir the liquid over a low heat or preferably in a heatproof bowl over gently simmering water until slightly thickened.

Place a layer of the rum-flavored macaroons in the bottom of a glass bowl and cover with a layer of the chocolate cream. Repeat these layers until the ingredients are finished, ending with a layer of chocolate cream. Chill overnight or longer if possible.

Serve from the bowl, with single cream if liked.

JP

Almond and Lemon Flan

A rich offering but usually irresistible. It can also be produced for a tea party.

FOR THE FLAN SHELL:
¼ cup all-purpose flour
pinch of salt
6 tablespoons (¾ stick) butter
¼ cup ground almonds
2 teaspoons lemon zest, grated
1 egg, beaten
a little water

FOR THE FILLING:
⅓ cup sugar
4 tablespoons (½ stick) butter, at room temperature
3 eggs
grated zest and juice of 2 lemons
1¼ cups ground almonds
1 teaspoon almond extract
⅔ cup heavy cream, whipped until thick
confectioners' sugar for sprinkling

To make the flan shell, sift the flour and salt together and rub in the butter until the mixture resembles fine crumbs. Stir in the ground almonds and lemon zest. Bind with the beaten egg, plus 1–2 teaspoons of water if necessary, to make a firm dough. Chill for half an hour, then roll out to line a 9-inch loose-bottomed tart pan. Chill once again for 20 minutes if possible.

Prick the bottom of the flan shell with a fork and line with parchment. Fill with dried beans and bake in a preheated oven at 350°F for 20 minutes. Remove the beans and parchment, then return to oven and bake for a further 10 minutes. Remove from the oven, and reduce the heat to 300°F.

For the filling, beat the sugar, butter, eggs and grated lemon zest together. Add the almonds, almond extract and lemon juice. Fold in the whipped cream and pour into the flan shell. Bake for about 40 minutes or until the filling is just set. Allow to cool, then dust the top with confectioners' sugar.

JP

Claret Jelly

This is a grown-up molded dessert. It has a wonderful color and smell and looks great turned from a complicated mold. I once made it before 150 of Edinburgh's finest, and so scared was I that it would not set that I added an extra gelatin leaf. It took me three goes to turn it out, which I finally did to the supportive cheers of the crowd! As always, the better the wine, the better the dessert.

2 envelopes unflavored gelatin
or 5 leaves gelatin
1 bottle Bordeaux-style wine
½ wine glass (2-2½ fluid ounces) brandy
1 small jar red-currant jelly
grated zest and juice 1 orange
¼ cup sugar

Soften the gelatin in a little cold water. Put all the remaining ingredients in a saucepan, bring to the boil and simmer for 10 minutes. Pour over the gelatin, stirring well until it is completely dissolved. Allow to cool slightly, then pour into a wetted 2½-pint mold. Chill until set. Turn out to serve (if you can, adds my friend, Isabel Rutherford).

CDW

Apple Amber Pudding

This is a meringue-topped flan, very comforting and friendly.

3–4 pounds tart apples, peeled, cored and sliced
½ cup granulated sugar
grated zest and juice of 1 lemon
2 eggs, separated
3 tablespoons (⅜ stick) unsalted butter, softened
½ pound refrigerated ready-made pie crust
⅓ cup sugar

Gently cook the apples with the granulated sugar until soft, then press through a sieve to purée. Add the lemon zest and juice. Beat in the egg yolks and butter. Line a 8-inch flan ring with the pastry, and pour in the apple mixture. Bake in a preheated oven at 375°F for 30 minutes. Reduce the oven temperature to 300°F.

Whisk the egg whites with the sugar until stiff but not dry. Spoon the meringue onto the apple filling, covering it completely. Bake for 15–20 minutes or until the meringue is pale brown.

CDW

Butterscotch Tart

When I was at school my father used to send me packets of butterscotch. I never knew why, but I became quite fond of butterscotch. This is another comforting pudding.

½ pound refrigerated ready-made pie crust
1 cup all-purpose flour
1 cup plus 2 tablespoons packed light brown sugar
⅔ cup water
⅔ cup warmed milk
6 tablespoons (¾ stick) unsalted butter
1 teaspoon vanilla extract
3 eggs, separated
⅓ cup sugar

Line an 8-inch tart pan with the pastry, and line with foil or parchment, weight with dried beans and bake blind in a preheated oven at 375°F for 30 minutes. Remove the pastry shell, and reduce the oven to 300°F.

Mix together the flour, brown sugar, water and milk in a saucepan and heat, stirring, until thickened. Remove from the heat and blend in the butter, vanilla and egg yolks. Pour into the tart shell. Whisk the egg whites with the sugar to form a meringue, and spoon on top of the filling to cover it completely. Bake for 15–20 minutes or until the meringue is lightly browned.

CDW

George Pudding

This is an eighteenth-century pudding, and probably a favorite of that pudding-eating monarch, George III. Considering the difficulties of his private life and the huge changes he witnessed in his lifetime, I'm not surprised he needed some consolation from puddings.

2½ cups milk
a strip of lemon zest
3 whole cloves
¼ cup long-grain rice
2 tablespoons sugar
2½ pounds stewed apples
⅔ cup dry white wine
2 tablespoons (¼ stick) butter
⅓ cup candied citrus peel, chopped
3 eggs, separated
two 8-inch pre-cooked puff pastry shells

Put the milk, lemon zest and cloves in a saucepan and bring to the boil. Add the rice and simmer for about 25-30 minutes until tender. Remove the cloves and lemon zest. Add the sugar, stewed apples, wine, butter, candied peel and egg yolks to the rice and stir to mix. Whisk the egg whites until stiff and fold into the mixture. Spoon into the vol-au-vent cases. Bake in a preheated oven at 350°F for about 35–40 minutes or until the filling is set and golden brown.

CDW

Chocolate Tart

Nearly everyone loves chocolate, so use the best you can find to make this terrific tart.

4 ounces bittersweet chocolate
2 tablespoons (¼ stick) butter
2 eggs
⅓ cup sugar
2 tablespoons all-purpose
flour, sifted
4 tablespoons heavy cream
1 8-inch tartlet shell, prebaked
whipped cream to decorate

Melt the chocolate with the butter, and leave to cool slightly. Whisk the eggs and sugar together until thick, then fold in the cooled chocolate mixture. Gently mix in the sifted flour and then the heavy cream. Pour into the pastry shell. Bake in a preheated oven at 350°F for 30 minutes or until the filling is lightly set. Leave to cool overnight, then decorate with piped whipped cream before serving.

JP

Fuggers' Lemon Cake

The Fuggers were an enormously wealthy South German family of merchant bankers, ennobled by the Emperor Maximilian in the sixteenth century. Their name was synonymous with taste and high living, as this recipe shows.

5 tablespoons (⅝ stick) butter
2 cups all-purpose flour
pinch of salt
1 egg plus 1 egg yolk
beaten egg or milk to glaze

FOR THE FILLING:
1⅔ cups ground almonds
4 tablespoons (½ stick) butter
½ cup sugar
grated zest of 1 lemon
juice of 2 lemons

Rub together the butter, flour and salt until crumb-like in texture. Add the egg, the additional egg yolk and a little cold water to bind to a dough. Chill for 1 hour. Use half the dough to line a 10-inch tart pan.

Combine all the filling ingredients in a bowl set over a pan of hot water, and mix to a smooth consistency. Pour into the pastry shell and cover with the remaining dough, sealing and fluting the edges. Brush the top with beaten egg or milk. Bake in a preheated oven at 425°F for 10 minutes, then reduce the heat to 350°F and bake for a further 30 minutes.

CDW

Rigo Jancsi Chocolate Slices

Before the days of unsavory "travelers", I wonder how many of us dreamed of running away "with the raggle taggle gypsies oh". Rigo Jansci could have been the model for the poem. He was a gypsy fiddler beloved of polite society (and boy, was it polite) in Budapest in the 1920s. Unfortunately it emerged that it was rather more than his music that was adored by the ladies, and a huge scandal ensued. An enterprising confectioner devised these delicious slices to cash in on the act. I owe this recipe and the story to a lady's maid who was there at the time.

3 eggs, separated
3 tablespoons sugar
1 ounce bittersweet chocolate, grated
2 tablespoons all-purpose flour

FOR THE FILLING:
apricot jam
¼ cup cocoa powder
¼ cup sugar
a few drops of vanilla extract
¾ cup heavy cream, stiffly whipped

FOR THE CHOCOLATE FROSTING:
3 ounces bittersweet chocolate
2 tablespoons (¼ stick) unsalted butter

Cream together the egg yolks and sugar. Whisk the egg whites until very stiff. Add the grated chocolate and flour to the yolk mixture, then fold in the egg whites. Line and grease a 1½-pound (9x5-inch) loaf pan and pour in the chocolate mixture. Bake in a preheated oven at 350°F for 15–20 minutes. Turn out and cool on a rack. When cold, slice in half lengthwise through the middle.

Spread both halves of cake with jam on the cut sides. For the filling, mix together all the remaining ingredients, and spread evenly over one half on top of the jam. Make the frosting by melting the chocolate with the butter. Allow to cool slightly, then spread over the jam on the other half. Set aside to cool until the chocolate sets. Put the two strips together so that the frosting and filling are together in the middle, with the frosted strip on top, and chill slightly before slicing to serve.

CDW

Aniseed Waffles

I had a spendid Belgian great-aunt whose measurement around her waist when she married was the same as the measurement around her neck when she died in her late 80s. These waffles were a great favorite at her house. If you do not have a waffle iron, either buy one, move on to the next recipe or try as cookies.

Makes 10–15

2 cups all-purpose flour
pinch of salt
¼ cup sugar
6 eggs
2 teaspoons aniseeds
1 tablespoon brandy

Sift the flour and salt into a bowl and add the sugar. Mix in the eggs one by one, then stir in the aniseeds and the brandy. Beat hard until well mixed (10 minutes by hand), then leave to rest for 5 hours.

Beat the batter again. Grease a hot electric waffle iron. Spread on a large spoonful of batter, close the iron and cook for 3–4 minutes or until the waffle is golden brown. These waffles will crisp up and keep well in an airtight tin.

CDW

Bread and Butter Pudding

I must admit that I am not fond of this much-loved pudding, but this is a very good way to make it, using stale croissants rather than bread.

2 stale croissants
softened butter
3 tablespoons golden raisins
⅓ cup sugar
2 eggs
1¾ cups half and half
grated lemon zest
freshly grated nutmeg

Slice and butter the croissants. Place in a buttered small gratin dish in layers, sprinkling the golden raisins and ¼ cup of the sugar between the layers. Beat the eggs with the remaining sugar. Bring the milk and cream just to the boil, and pour on to the egg mixture. Mix well together, then strain into a bowl and add the grated lemon zest. Pour the custard over the layered croissants and leave to stand for 1 hour before baking.

Place the dish in a baking pan containing enough hot water to come half way up the dish. Grate a little nutmeg over the top of the pudding and bake in a preheated oven at 325°F for about 45 minutes or until the custard is set.

JP

Sussex Pond Pudding

The lemon should burst inside this pudding, creating the "pond" when you cut into it.

1½ cups all-purpose flour
¼ cup sugar
6 tablespoons solid vegetable shortening
pinch of salt
1 egg, beaten
grated zest and juice of 1 lemon

FOR THE FILLING:
1 small thin-skinned lemon
⅓ cup sugar
6 tablespoons (¾ stick) unsalted butter

Place the flour, sugar, shortening and salt in a large bowl. Cut in the fat until the mixture resembles crumbs. Add the beaten egg, lemon zest and a few tablespoons of lemon juice to make a light dough. Use about two-thirds of the dough to line a buttered 4–5 cup pudding mold or souffle dish, coming about 1 inch up the sides.

Make incisions at ½-inch intervals all over the lemon. Combine the butter and sugar and place in the center of the lined mold. Nestle the lemon in it. Cover with a lid of the remaining dough, pressing the edges together to seal. Wrap the mold with a dishcloth and tie over the top with string. Set in a pan of simmering water, cover and steam for 2½ hours, watching the level of water in the pan.

CDW

Small Banana Soufflés

Try these charming soufflés for a children's party. They will love them and it will be a change from the usual party fare.

FOR THE PASTRY CREAM:
1 egg yolk
1 tablespoon all-purpose flour
3 tablespoons milk
5 teaspoons sugar

4 large bananas
1 egg yolk
5 teaspoons sugar
½ teaspoon vanilla extract
a few drops of lemon juice
2 egg whites

To make the pastry cream mix the egg yolk, flour, milk and sugar together in a small saucepan. When the mixture is smooth, put over a moderate heat and bring to the boil, stirring. Simmer for a few seconds, still stirring, then remove the saucepan from the heat.

Mash the bananas until *very* smooth (or put through a sieve), then stir in the egg yolk, sugar, vanilla extract and lemon juice. Fold in the pastry cream. Beat the egg whites until stiff and fold into the mixture. Turn into four buttered and sugared ramekin dishes and bake in a preheated oven at 375°F for 10–15 minutes. Serve immediately.

JP

Granita of Prosecco with Sliced Blood Oranges

This beautiful and refreshing concoction is simplicity itself to make, but it is worth taking the time and care to remove each segment of orange from its pith and skin. If you can't get blood oranges you can, of course, use ordinary oranges, but the result isn't quite so stunning. I suppose you could add some pretend blood with the aid of a little cassis.

1 bottle of prosecco or other sparkling wine
6–8 blood oranges (1½–2 per person)
sugar to taste

Pour the sparkling wine into a plastic container with a lid and put it into a freezer. As the wine freezes, keep taking it out and mixing it to get a granular look. Don't let it solidify into a block.

Peel the oranges with a very sharp small knife, removing all the skin and pith, then cut each segment free from its skin. Arrange the segments in elegant glass bowls, sprinkle with as much sugar as you want and top with spoonfuls of the granita glowing like diamonds on a sunset. Fab.

JP

Gooseberry and Elderflower Parfait

This parfait is rather a treat as gooseberries don't have a very long season, although you can purée them in quantities and freeze. The purée is also useful to serve with mackerel.

½ pound gooseberries
6 tablespoons water
½ cup sugar
4 egg yolks
2 tablespoons elderflower cordial
⅔ cup heavy cream, whipped until thick

TO SERVE:
whipped cream flavored with elderflower cordial

Simmer the gooseberries with 3 tablespoons of the water until soft. When tender pureé the gooseberries, and then strain the purée through a sieve. Very gently heat the sugar with the remaining water until the sugar has dissolved, then bring to the boil and simmer for 2–3 minutes. Remove from the heat. Place the egg yolks in a large bowl and whisk together. While whisking, gradually pour on the sugar syrup, and continue whisking until the mixture is very thick and cold. Whisk in the elderflower cordial, then fold in the lightly whipped cream and the gooseberry purée. Pour the mixture into a 3½x7½x2¼-inch loaf pan lined with plastic wrap and freeze until solid, preferably overnight if possible.

About 15–20 minutes before serving, turn out onto a serving dish and leave to soften in the refrigerator. Then cut into slices. Put a blob of elderflower-flavored whipped cream at the side of each serving.

JP

Illustrated overleaf

BREAKFASTS

Driving a bike and sidecar is hard enough, without a cameraman in front of you

CLARISSA WRITES: Every nutritionist I have ever met agrees that breakfast is the most important meal of the day. Night is the longest period of time we go without food; in the morning we have the whole day in front of us and we need energy to tackle it. So what do we do? We stagger downstairs, grab a cup of something hot and probably instant and if we eat at all, it is probably cereal – with semi-skimmed milk even though the body cannot absorb the calcium in the milk without the fat, and osteoporosis is on the increase – or a swift piece of toast eaten on the run.

Jennifer says that after a bracing dip in the briny, breakfast is very welcome and she likes yogurt for the digestion and hangovers, fruit for regularity and a perfectly-poached egg. Dr Johnson, well known for his love of the Scots, said, "If a man would breakfast well, he should breakfast in Scotland." Think of Scotland's gifts to the meal: oatmeal porridge (which has recently saved me from the need for a surgical operation); cold smoked fish; fillets of undyed haddock cooked with milk; and, of course, marmalade. The whole Spanish Seville orange crop is now reserved for the British marmalade market.

We have found out the hard way how difficult it is to find a good breakfast on the road. In one hotel, my poached eggs were served in a demi-lune salad dish, without toast but with a amount of salt. Unsurprisingly our host, Mr Peacock, is a Scot. What can beat a good breakfast, even if the face on the other side of the table is Jennifer's and not that of the man of my dreams. We are very jolly for it and sally forth to mob up the world in a much happier frame of mind. Even the Black Prince, our motorbike, responds to our mood. As I write, we are off to cook lunch for a motorcyle rally, the sun is shining, and I can smell the coffee which Rex Phillips, our beloved sound man, brings us every morning. Breakfast beckons for us, as I hope it will for you too.

Jennifer demonstrates the importance of having a sharp knife to hand at all times

bunch of watercress and a free ant, to much ribald laughter from us! We have had eggs cooked in some tasteless, amorphous, artificial fat and tasting like blotting paper, and bacon which disgraced the poor pig who gave his all.

Currently we are staying at Boltongate Rectory, a Wolsey Lodge in Cumbria, and what a joy the breakfast is. Nothing can surpass a well-laid breakfast table, and here the porridge is smooth and delicious and the eggs golden with proud yolks, while the bacon has just the right

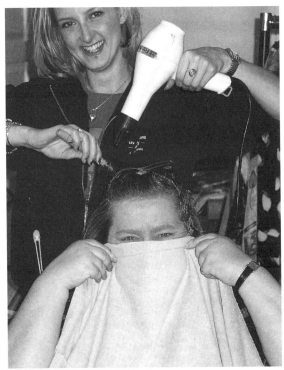

Clarissa prepares for another filming session with the help of her "visagist"

Fruit Porridge

I feel rather like a crusader returning from Outremer to discover that the Holy Grail had been sitting on my own mantlepiece all along. I was raised on porridge. It was a daily feature of our breakfast table, and my father railed at me for eating it with sugar rather than in the Scot's fashion with salt. So I abandoned porridge for what I saw as sophistication. As a recovering alcoholic I have, as so many of us do, the legacy of a colic gut. The combination of that with the stresses of being catapulted overnight into a TV success, and adhesions on an old operation scar, kept laying me low in agony. To Harley Street I went. Amidst all the words of wisdom I received, one struck a true chord: try eating porridge. I am happy to report that having done so on a daily basis for a month I have been so well and happy that I am in danger of becoming an evangelist.

There are different types of oats and oatmeal. Rolled oats, which make a more textured porridge, need to be soaked first. Fine oatmeal, which is added to boiling water, makes the easiest porridge, but perhaps the least textured. Whichever oats you use, the important thing to remember is not to let the mixture stick to the bottom of the pan, as there is nothing quite so nasty as burnt porridge. To this end I always cook it in a double boiler. In the Glasgow slums they used to make porridge once a week and pour it into a drawer, then cut off a piece as they needed it. I have yet to try this. One of my best friends is Swedish, and she tells me that the Swedes, unlike the Calvinistic Scots, enhance their porridge with berries. In winter they add dried blueberries, cloudberries or cranberries to the last few minutes of the cooking process, and in season they add fresh berries or chopped apple after the porridge is cooked.

5 cups water
1 cup rolled oats (not instant)
salt
2 tablespoons dried berries or other fruit
milk, cream, or buttermilk

Bring the water to the boil, then rain in the oatmeal, stirring. When the porridge is boiling steadily, reduce the heat, cover and simmer for 35–40 minutes, stirring intermittently. Add salt to taste and the fruit 5 minutes before the end of the cooking time. Serve with milk, cream or buttermilk. In Scotland the milk is served in a separate small bowl into which each spoonful of porridge is dipped.

CDW

Proper Scrambled Eggs

Apart from the omelet, eggs should be cooked slowly or they toughen. Think of those bullet-like fried eggs surrounded by black lace so beloved in the old transport cafes, or pub boiled eggs in vinegar with the consistency of rubber. This also calls to mind bought Scotch eggs, the scrambled eggs left in a chafing dish on the sideboard, a congealed yellow blancmange sitting in a pool of condensed water — all terrible and all to be avoided. Breakfast is really one of the most difficult things to prepare as all the ingredients require different times of cooking. This method of scrambling eggs not only produces a lovely creamy mass of eggs, but lets you get on with other things. I reckon about 3 eggs per person for a hearty helping, and I have yet to find that I have prepared too much.

Serves 4–6

12 eggs minus 3 of the whites
1 egg shell of water
salt and freshly ground pepper
½ cup (1 stick) unsalted butter
hot toast

Use a double boiler, porringer or simply a heatproof bowl set over simmering water. The eggs should be as fresh as possible, of course. Beat the eggs and water together very well and season with salt and lots of freshly ground pepper. Melt the butter in the top of the double boiler or bowl, pour in the eggs and give them a stir. Then you can get on with your other preparations for breakfast, just keeping an eye on the eggs and stirring every now and then to keep them creamy. When they have reached the consistency you require (this can take 15–20 minutes), pile them on to hot toast and serve with bacon, sausages or what you will.

JP

Eggs Benedict

The receipt for this dish originated in America, where it is served on so-called "English muffins". It was named for a patron of the Waldorf Astoria Hotel, New York, whose favorite form of eggs it was. These eggs also make a very good luncheon dish.

4 slices of cooked ham
butter
4 slices of white bread
4 eggs
hollandaise sauce

Lightly fry the cooked ham in a buttered frying pan. Toast the bread slices and butter them. Poach the eggs. Put the ham on top of the toast and the poached eggs on the ham, and spoon over some warm hollandaise sauce. Serve straight away.

JP

Fried Eggs on Puffball Mushrooms

Giant puffball mushrooms are now very popular in some London restaurants. They are also very expensive because people have become more aware of them and they are thus difficult to get hold of. They are in season during high summer, rather earlier than the ordinary field mushroom. Puffballs were considered a great delicacy in days gone by and were served up on state occasions. However, they went out of fashion as fungi became suspect. If you see these amazing fungi in the country, pick them up at once as they tend to turn to powder when old.

puffball mushrooms
5 eggs, 1 beaten
fresh bread crumbs
butter
fresh lemon juice

To prepare puffballs, cut them as you would slice bread. Dip the slices in the beaten egg and then bread crumbs, pressing on firmly, and leave to rest for half an hour. Then sauté the slices in some butter, turning once. Remove to a platter and fry the eggs in some more butter. Serve with a dash of lemon juice and a fried egg on top.

JP

Corn Griddle Cakes

My mother was a great devotee of all things relating to the Southern States of America. After a dose of Francis Parkinson Keyes she would drive the cook mad with requests for recipes from "Dixie," so with a cry of "company's a comin' Miz Scarlett," the cook would retire to make these griddle cakes for breakfast in the hopes that my father might object. He never did as he liked them, so we had them quite often. Finally, one of my sisters married a man from South Carolina, which cured my mother of her Dixie obsession. These should be cooked on a griddle, but if you do not have one, a heavy frying pan will do.

2 cups all-purpose flour
1½ teaspoons baking powder
¼ teaspoon paprika
½ teaspoon salt
6 ounces fresh corn kernels
cut from the cob (frozen or
canned will do)
1 egg, beaten
½ cup milk
2 tablespoons melted butter

Sift the dry ingredients into a bowl. Combine the corn, egg and milk, add to the flour mixture and mix well. Then add the butter. Spoon onto a hot griddle, using 2 or 3 tablespoons of the mixture for each cake. Cook until bubbles show on the surface, then turn the cakes over and cook the other sides until golden brown. Serve with crisp slices of bacon and maple syrup, if liked.

CDW

Huevos Rancheros

I love this dish for breakfast, and am delighted to see that my friend, Caroline Brett, the brilliant young restaurateur, is serving it for breakfast at the Union Café in Marylebone Lane, London.

Serves 6

corn oil
6 corn tortillas (6-inch diameter)
12 eggs

FOR THE GREEN CHILE SAUCE:
½ pound coarsely ground lean beef
2 cups water
2 medium tomatoes, chopped
1 large roasted green chile, chopped
½ onion, finely chopped
1 garlic clove, crushed
dash of Worcestershire sauce
salt and freshly ground pepper
2 tablespoons cornstarch
refried beans

To make the chile sauce, brown the beef in a little oil over medium heat. Add all the other ingredients, except the cornstarch, and stir. Bring to the boil, then simmer for 10–15 minutes. Add the cornstarch (mixed with a little water), stir well and cook for 10 minutes more. (The sauce keeps in the fridge and can be frozen. It may need more liquid if too thick after thawing.) Keep the sauce hot.

Heat 1–2 tablespoons of oil in a large frying pan and shallow fry the tortillas, one at a time, for a few seconds on each side (be careful they don't become crisp). Drain on paper towels. Pour off most of the oil, then return the pan to a low heat. Fry the eggs 2 or 3 at a time. Top each tortilla with 2 eggs and pour a ladle of green chile sauce over each portion. Serve with refried beans.

CDW

Oeufs en Cocotte (Baked Eggs)

We used to love these as children, probably because we got our own little pots, sometimes covered in shredded cheese and put under the broiler.

Serves 6

3 tablespoons (⅜ stick) butter
6 tablespoons heavy cream
6 large fresh eggs
salt and freshly ground black pepper
1 heaping tablespoon chopped fresh chives or tarragon

Use 2 tablespoons of the butter to grease six cocottes or ramekin dishes. Warm the cream and put a tablespoonful in each dish. Break an egg carefully into each dish. Sprinkle with salt, pepper and chives or tarragon and dot with the remaining butter. Place the dishes in a large roasting pan and pour hot water into the pan until it comes half way up the dishes. Bake in a preheated oven at 375°F for 7–8 minutes. The yolks should still be soft — remember that they will keep on cooking in their little dishes until eaten.

JP

Omelet Arnold Bennett

In the Edwardian era it was very fashionable to name dishes after prominent people. Escoffier, during his sojourn at the Savoy Hotel (from which he was sacked for fiddling the egg account), was a dab hand at this, and one of his most successful dishes was named after the novelist and theatre critic Arnold Bennett. I am writing this at Kinloch Lodge Hotel on the Isle of Skye, where today I have stood as godmother at the confirmation of Godfrey Macdonald, hereditary Lord of the Isles, for all that Prince Charles tries to poach his title. His wife, Claire, is not only a great friend, but also a splendid cook, and I am giving her my version of this dish which includes tomatoes.

1 pound smoked haddock
4 cups milk
4 tablespoons (½ stick) butter
½ cup all-purpose flour
½ cup Parmesan cheese, freshly grated
1 tablespoon finely chopped parsley
2 tomatoes, peeled, seeded and chopped
freshly ground black pepper
freshly grated nutmeg
8 eggs
butter for frying
4 tablespoons heavy cream

Poach the fish gently in the milk for 5 minutes, then remove from the heat and leave to cool in the milk. Remove the fish and flake into a dish, discarding all skin and bones. Strain the milk and reserve 2½ cups.

Make a white sauce with the butter, flour and reserved milk according to the procedure on page 149. Mix in the flaked fish, cheese, parsley, tomatoes, and pepper and nutmeg to taste.

Make an omelet with 2 of the eggs. When the underside is set, put a portion of the fish mixture on top and let it warm through. The underside of the omelet will now be golden brown. Pour over 1 tablespoon cream and place the omelet under a preheated hot broiler for 2 minutes. Serve on a hot plate without folding. Make three more omelets in the same way.

CDW

Deviled Kidneys

Deviled kidneys were very popular in Victorian days, but seem to have suffered a decline in more recent times. Lamb's kidneys, being milder than ox or pig's kidneys, are favored for this dish. Use a light hand when cooking kidneys — over cooked they become nasty, like little bits of leather.

2 teaspoons Worcestershire sauce
2 teaspoons mushroom catsup (available at specialty stores)
1 level teaspoon dry mustard powder
4 tablespoons melted butter
pinch of cayenne pepper
salt and freshly ground pepper
8 lamb's kidneys
1 tablespoon vegetable oil
1 teaspoons chopped parsley
lemon wedges
hot buttered toast

Mix together the Worcestershire sauce, mushroom catsup, mustard, 2 tablespoons of the melted butter, the cayenne pepper, and a seasoning of salt and pepper. Clean the kidneys by removing the outer skin and cutting away the core. Cut each kidney into three or four pieces. Heat the remaining butter with the oil in a frying pan and cook the kidneys for 4–5 minutes, turning occasionally. Pour the sauce mixture over the kidneys and stir for 1–2 minutes to coat the kidneys.

Serve on warmed plates, sprinkled with a little parsley and accompanied by lemon wedges and hot buttered toast.

JP

Illustrated overleaf

Bloody Mary

I think this is more for a brunch than early breakfast, when it could seriously damage your day.

Quantities per person

1 jigger (1½ ounces) of vodka
2 dashes of Worcestershire
sauce
a dash of lemon juice
a few drops of hot-pepper
sauce
pinch each of salt and freshly
ground pepper
ice cubes
tomato juice

Place the vodka, Worcestershire sauce, lemon juice, hot-pepper sauce, salt and pepper in a small glass. Add ice cubes and fill up with tomato juice. Stir well and serve.

JP

Ham 'n' Haddie

One of Scotland's greatest contributions to the enjoyment of food is cold smoked fish, and the pale opalescent hue of an undyed smoked haddock on the breakfast table is a great joy. Finnan haddies take their name from Findon in Kincardineshire, where the fish wives hung their dried salted haddocks in their chimneys to smoke over their peat fires. A Finnan haddie is a whole cured fish, bones and all, and is the smoked haddock to use for this dish. It is a traditional Scot's breakfast dish, which can equally well be eaten for high tea.

Serves 6

2 tablespoons (¼ stick) butter
2 large slices of cooked ham, cut from the bone
2 large smoked haddock
⅔ cup milk
freshly ground black pepper
⅔ cup heavy cream

Heat the butter in a large pan and lightly fry the ham, turning once; remove and cut into six pieces. Place the haddock in the pan and cover with the milk. Bring to the boil and simmer for 2 minutes on each side. Lift out the fish, remove skin and bones, and divide the flesh into six pieces. Strain the milk and reserve. Return the ham to the pan, place the haddock pieces on top and gently pour over the milk. Season with pepper. Cover and simmer gently for 3 minutes. Pour the cream evenly over the surface, and brown under a preheated broiler.

CDW

Mustard Bloaters

I love bloaters, which are whole ungutted herrings, as distinct from kippers which are split down the back. When Clara Peggotty in *David Copperfield* describes herself as a Yarmouth bloater, Dickens is implying that she is plump, juicy and well preserved. Bloaters were a new delicacy at the time (the cure was perfected in 1835), and because the herring was only half dried before smoking, they remained plump and puffed out. Their lighter cure means they do not keep as well as kippers and should be eaten when bought; however, in this age of refrigeration that is no problem, and we should all clamour for the wider availability of the bloater (I remember when you could only buy olive oil in pharmacies – public demand is a great mover of mountains).

Bloaters are also very good deviled. Broil them as described here, but spread with a mixture of prepared mustard, chutney, lemon juice, salt, and sugar.

4 bloaters
1 tablespoon freshly made English mustard
4 tablespoons butter, melted, or 2 tablespoons oil
3 tablespoons toasted bread crumbs

Preheat the broiler. Clean and trim the bloaters, and make diagonal slashes along one side of each fish. Brush with butter or oil and broil lightly on both sides. Fill the slashes with mustard, sprinkle with bread crumbs and pour over the rest of the butter or oil. Return to the broiler, crumbed side up, and cook until brown, crisp and cooked through.

CDW

Herrings in Oatmeal and Mustard with Bacon

We know herrings are full of the important fish oils so dear to the heart of doctors and to the heart itself. They are still cheap, they are wonderful to eat and they are available to all, so why do people not eat more of them in this country, apart from the Scots? This is a fine method used in Scotland, which could be eaten for any meal. The mustard is my idea, as I have always found it goes well with oily fish.

Serves 6

¾ cup fine or medium oatmeal
1 tablespoons dry mustard powder
6 lovely fresh herrings, boned
salt and freshly ground black pepper
12 slices of first-class bacon
⅔ cup bacon drippings or lard
parsley, chopped
lemon wedges

Mix the oatmeal with the mustard on a large platter or board. Season the herrings with salt and pepper, and press firmly into the oatmeal mixture, coating well on both sides. Fry the bacon in the fat or lard until crisp, then drain on paper towels. Keep warm while you fry the herrings in the fat until nicely browned, about 3 minutes on each side, turning them carefully to keep the oatmeal in place. Serve the herrings with the bacon and a little scattering of parsley. Lemon wedges are a good addition to cut the fat. Do not eat the skins.

JP

Kedgeree

Hindi "khichri," the original kedgeree, is a dish of boiled rice and lentils. I imagine a little Bombay duck (a sort of Indian dried fish) was added at some point to give the fishy part, and when the dish was brought home to England by some old colonel at the beginning of the nineteenth century, smoked haddock was substituted. Kedgeree became the mainstay of Victorian breakfasts, with the lentils eschewed entirely and eggs added. It is the most comforting dish in the world.

Serves 4–6

1 pound smoked haddock
1 medium onion, finely chopped
½ cup (1 stick) butter
1 teaspoon garam masala
½ teaspoon turmeric
1½ cups basmati rice
4 hard-cooked eggs, 2 roughly chopped and 2 quartered
1½ cups cream, warmed (optional)
salt and freshly ground pepper
1 tablespoon chopped parsley

Simmer the haddock in 2 quarts of salted water for 10–15 minutes, but don't overcook. Drain the fish, saving the cooking water. Remove the skin and bones, and flake the fish; keep hot. Fry the onion gently in the butter with the garam masala and turmeric until softened. Cook the rice in the haddock water until tender, then drain and allow to dry out a little. Add the spiced fried onion to the rice, and fold in the flaked fish and the roughly chopped eggs. Pour in the cream and add the quartered eggs. Season with salt and pepper, and sprinkle the parsley over all.

JP

A Sefton of Herring Roes

This dish was designed in the 1860s as a savoury for the Earl of Sefton of the day, who was a rakehell of great elegance. I was introduced to it by a man who, as a junior boy at Harrow school, had fagged (acted as an unpaid servant) for Sefton's grandson and used to make it for his breakfast. This dish is served chilled and is excellent for a summer's breakfast.

½ pound soft herring roes
1 tablespoon lemon juice
salt and freshly ground pepper
2 tablespoons (¼ stick) butter
4 tablespoons heavy cream
3 anchovy fillets, chopped
1 teaspoon capers
water biscuits
cayenne pepper
watercress

Season the roes with the lemon juice, salt and pepper. Fry in the butter briefly, then blend to a soft pulp. Whip the cream and blend into the pulp with the anchovies and capers. Chill. Serve on water biscuits garnished with cayenne pepper and watercress.

CDW

Jugged Kippers

The great thing about this method of cooking kippers is that it doesn't stink the house out, and I think the result far more succulent than broiled kippers. Make sure you get naturally smoked kippers. Manx or Arbroath are both good, although Manx has the lighter smoke. Loch Fyne are wonderful.

kippers
butter
lemons

Cut the heads and tails off the kippers. Put them in a jug, head end first, and pour boiling water into the jug to fill it, making sure the kippers remain upright. Cover the jug with a plate and leave for 4–5 minutes. Pour off the water, and put the kippers on the plate with a ½ tablespoon of butter and a lemon wedge each. Eat some bread and butter with it — it helps the bones go down! Good brown bread and unsalted butter are best.

JP

Cumberland Shipped Herring

My father grew up in Glasgow where Loch Fyne herrings, which were the fattest and best, were known as Glasgow Magistrates. Thanks to my friend, Johnny Noble, Loch Fyne herrings are once again flourishing. If you are driving up the west coast of Scotland don't miss a stop at Johnny's seafood restaurant at Cairndow; it is worth a detour.

As a child, I used to go to the West of Scotland for holidays, and herrings were staple fare. This dish is from Cumberland, further down the west coast, a strange remote area that until 1294 was part of Scotland and which remained very remote until Victorian times. Herrings are now hard to come by unless asked for in your fishmonger (not supermarket). Remember, they are very good for you.

4 fresh herrings
4 herring roes
¼ cup bread crumbs
2 teaspoons anchovy extract
1 small onion, chopped
1 tablespoon melted butter
salt and freshly ground pepper
4 tablespoons (½ stick) butter

Clean the herrings, and remove heads, tails, fins and backbones (a fishmonger will do this for you). Gently poach the herring roes in hot water for a few minutes. Drain and chop, then mix with the bread crumbs, anchovy extract, onion, melted butter and seasoning to taste. Stuff the herrings with the mixture and secure each with a wooden cocktail stick. Lay the fish side by side in a buttered baking dish and dot with the butter. Bake in a preheated oven at 350°F for about 20 minutes.

CDW

Salmon Fish Cakes

Always a great favorite with school boys (or the grown-up ones). It's worth buying a piece of salmon and cooking it specially to make the fish cakes instead of just using left overs.

14 ounces cooked salmon
1 cup unseasoned mashed potatoes
1 egg yolk
2 ounces smoked salmon, cut into tiny pieces
a little parsley, chopped
2 tablespoons melted butter plus more for frying
salt and freshly ground pepper
1 egg, beaten
bread crumbs

Remove the skin and bones from the salmon, and mash the fish coarsely. Add the mashed potatoes, the egg yolk, smoked salmon, chopped parsley, melted butter, salt and pepper. Shape into round, flat cakes. Dip in beaten egg and then coat with bread crumbs. Fry the fish cakes in hot butter until golden brown on both sides.

JP

Red Flannel Hash

I was always much too snooty to eat corned beef hash until I met a young man named Paul, sadly now dead, who made the most delicious hash which he ate for most meals including breakfast. Later I came across this recipe from the southern states of America which is made with roast beef instead. The name comes from the hue imparted by the beets, which resembles the color of red flannel underwear, presumably a suitable garb for breakfasting in.

12 ounces cold roast beef, chopped
1 pound boiled potatoes, chopped
1 cooked beet, chopped
1 small onion, chopped
1 egg, beaten with 1 tablespoon milk
1 teaspoon horseradish sauce (available from specialty stores)
salt and freshly ground pepper
2 tablespoons (¼ stick) butter

Mix together all the ingredients except the butter, seasoning to taste. Melt the butter in a heavy frying pan. Spread the mixture evenly in the pan and cook slowly until browned on the underside. Serve with fried eggs.

CDW

TEAS

*"Sandwiches before cake, gentlemen." Jennifer and Clarissa serve up tea
at the Warborough Cricket Club*

CLARISSA WRITES: Tea is not a meal Jennifer enjoys. I feel she rather thinks she has grown out of it. She does, however, reminisce enthusiastically over a high tea she ate in Scotland during the war. Coming straight from the deprivations of rationing, the large pats of white butter, the luscious ham with its gleaming fat, the fresh eggs and the plates of sweet offerings all made a great impression. I also remember teas like that, served on a snowy cloth, the scones hot and fragrant and all the baked goods smelling of fruit and cinnamon and spices; the home-made jams shining like jewels and the great black pot of tea dispensing good cheer. For me it was not wartime, and I came

from a home with a lavish table, but I will never forget the beauty of a Scottish high tea.

Tea comes in all shapes and sizes: there is the massive high tea, which is really supper, and suggested recipes for which you will find in the Light Dishes, Appetizers, and Savories chapter of this book. Then there is tea served with dainty sandwiches and gooey cakes in an English country garden with a silver teapot on a silver tray, damask napkins and the plink of tennis balls offstage. I feel sorry for people who never set foot out of London and so do not realise that this world still exists.

For the programme, we chose to create a cricket tea. I grew up in the shadow of Lord's

LEFT *An idyllic scene: the cricketers enjoy their tea*

BELOW *Another gentleman takes an interest: Mike Holden of Warborough Cricket Club welcomes Jennifer and Clarissa*

cricket ground and spent my holidays sitting in the Secretary's private box watching Middlesex with devotion and adoration. Money and television have ruined cricket at top level for me, but I still find great happiness watching village sides. I am an accredited umpire, though I add new meaning to the term "wide" these days.

For me, a day watching cricket with devoted wives and girlfriends bringing cakes and sandwiches embodies a lot that is still good about England. They have ruined tea at the Ritz, cream teas too often come with artificial cream out of a spray can, and sandwiches come too thickly cut, with the crusts left on. I once knew a wonderful woman who had been a lady's maid and made delicious, wafer-thin tomato sandwiches which were well worth the effort. For me, a cricketing tea is the thing any day.

The tea itself is important. I hate teabags: Jennifer says used ones are very good for the eyes and you should keep them cold in the refrigerator, but I would rather use the remains of the cucumber from the sandwiches. Forget your hippy herbals, tea should be Indian, made in a silver pot and served with milk and sugar, or China, made in a fine bone-china teapot and served with a wafer-thin slice of lemon. On location we have horrid polystyrene cups, but whilst filming in Cumbria we ate excellent bacon sandwiches from the well-known van on the Devil's Bridge at Kirkby Lonsdale and I am glad to say that the accompanying tea came in china mugs;

Honey Picnic Cake

If you go down to the woods today, take one of these along as a present. You will no doubt be made most welcome.

½ cup (1 stick) butter, at room temperature
⅓ cup dark brown sugar, packed
6 eggs, separated
2 cups self-rising flour
pinch of salt
1 teaspoon ground cinnamon
1 teaspoon pumpkin pie spice
⅔ cup dark honey
¾ cup plus 2 tablespoons chopped walnuts

Cream the butter and sugar together well. Gradually beat in the egg yolks, then add the honey. Sift the flour, salt and spices together and add gradually to the mixture. Fold in the walnuts. Whisk the egg whites until stiff and fold gently into the mixture.

Turn into a well-greased 8-inch cake pan. Bake in a preheated oven at 375°F for about 50–60 minutes. Test with a metal skewer and touch the top to test for springiness.

JP

Dalmatian Custard Cake

The Emperor Diocletian, who retired to Dalmatia to grow cabbages, no doubt enjoyed this cake, so venerable is its history.

5 cups milk
1 cup semolina
pinch of salt
½ cup (1 stick) butter
6 eggs
¾ cup sugar
1 teaspoon vanilla extract
1 cup raisins soaked in rum
2 cups shelled walnuts, roughly chopped

Bring the milk to the boil, then add the semolina and stir until thick. Add the salt and butter. Remove from the heat and stir in the eggs, sugar and vanilla. Add the raisins with 1 tablespoon of the rum and the walnuts. Spread in a well-buttered pie plate. Bake in a preheated oven at 350°F for 45 minutes or until firm.

CDW

Chocolate Whisky Cake

Not much whisky here, but enough to give taste to a lovely cake.

½ cup golden raisins

4 tablespoons Scotch whisky

6 ounces bittersweet chocolate

½ cup (1 stick) butter or margarine

3 eggs, separated

¾ cup packed brown sugar

½ cup chopped walnuts

zest of 1 small orange, grated

½ cup self-rising flour

¼ teaspoon freshly grated nutmeg

FOR THE TOPPING:

4 tablespoons (½ stick) unsalted butter, at room temperature

1¼ cups confectioners' sugar, sifted

4 tablespoons Scotch whisky

Soak the golden raisins in the whisky for several hours, preferably overnight. Melt the chocolate and butter very gently in a heatproof bowl set over a pan of barely simmering water, then leave to cool. Beat the egg yolks with the sugar until pale and thick. Fold in the cooled chocolate mixture, golden raisins with any remaining whisky, the walnuts and grated orange zest. Add the flour and nutmeg and fold in gently. Whisk the egg whites until stiff and fold into the cake batter. Spoon into a greased 8-inch cake pan. Bake in the center of a preheated oven at 350°F for 1 hour, or until a skewer inserted in the center of the cake comes out clean. Leave in the pan for 15 minutes, then turn out on to a wire rack and leave to cool.

For the topping, cream the butter and sugar together until smooth. Add the whisky and beat until it has been absorbed. Spread over the top of the cake.

JP

Apricot Shortcakes

The recipe for these good little cakes comes from the late Michael Smith.

Makes 20–22

1½ cups all-purpose flour
½ cup (1 stick) unsalted butter
2 ounces ground rice
(uncooked rice ground in a
coffee or spice grinder)
¼ cup sugar
4 tablespoons apricot jam

Sift the flour into a bowl and rub in the butter to the texture of fine bread crumbs. Add the ground rice and sugar and mix well. Put 2 tablespoons apricot jam in the center of the mixture and work into a smooth dough.

Roll out to ¼ inch thick and cut into 2-inch rounds. Place on greased baking sheets. With a thimble make a small hollow in the middle of each cookie and place a little jam in each. Bake in a preheated oven at 350°F for 20 minutes. Cool on a wire rack.

CDW

Orange Gobbet Cakes

How language changes. A gobbet is an eighteenth-century word for a mouthful, a polite and dainty word, perfect to describe these little cakes.

Makes 4 dozen

½ cup (1 stick) unsalted butter, at room temperature
¼ cup sugar
finely grated zest and juice of 1 orange
1½ cups self-rising flour
1 teaspoon baking powder
2 eggs, beaten
4 pieces of stem ginger in syrup, drained and cut into slivers

Cream the butter with the sugar and orange zest. Sift the flour with the baking powder. Mix the flour and beaten eggs alternately into the creamed mixture. Add enough orange juice to give the mixture a dropping consistency.

Butter the smallest tartlet pans and spoon in the mixture. Put a sliver of ginger on each. Bake in a preheated oven at 375°F for 15 minutes or until done.

CDW

Carrotts' Oatmeal Bars

In the distant days when we were starving school girls, I made two friends who have lasted me my life through to date. One of them, Caroline Driver, nicknamed Carrotts, became an instant favorite because she brought with her the most delicious oatmeal bars I have ever eaten. It put me off anyone else's for life. More years down the line than either of us would willingly admit to, she has given me the recipe.

Makes 16

¾ cup Demerara sugar
¾ cup (1½ sticks) butter
1⅓ cups rolled oats
pinch of salt

Melt the sugar and butter together in a saucepan. Mix in the oats and salt. Pour the mixture into a greased and lined 8 x 12 inch baking pan, and press firmly down into the tin to flatten evenly.

Bake in the center of a preheated oven at 350°F for 30 minutes. When cooked, cut into 16 fingers and leave to cool in the pan. Store in an airtight container.

CDW

Brandy Snaps

Like pancakes, the first brandy snaps you make are a bit ragged, but don't despair. You will get better and better.

Makes about 20

4 tablespoons (½ stick) butter
2 tablespoons light corn syrup
¼ cup sugar
½ cup all-purpose flour
1 level teaspoon ground ginger
⅔ cup heavy cream
2 teaspoons brandy

Put the butter, light corn syrup and sugar into a saucepan and heat gently until melted. Remove from the heat, and stir in the flour and ginger. Grease 2 or 3 cooking sheets thoroughly with butter. Put teaspoonfuls of the mixture on the cooking sheets, about 3 inches apart to allow for spreading. Bake in a preheated oven at 325°F for 8–10 minutes or until golden brown. Keep an eye on them to make sure they do not get too brown.

In the meantime grease the handle of a wooden spoon. Remove the cooking sheets from the oven and leave the cookies to cool for 2–3 minutes. Then, one at a time, lift them off with a palette knife and roll and press around the wooden spoon. Hold until the snap is set, then slide it off on to a wire rack. If the cookies become too stiff to roll, return them to the oven briefly to warm and soften.

Whip the cream and add the brandy. Pipe a dollop of cream into each snap.

JP

Fresh Fruit Tartlets

Fancy is as fancy does, and nothing could be fancier than little fruit tartlets. They are good and messy, but a pleasure to the eye and taste.

Makes about 10

4 ounces refrigerated ready-made pie crust
2 ounces bittersweet chocolate, melted
½ cup cream cheese, at room temperature
1 tablespoon heavy cream
3 teaspoons sugar
a few drops of vanilla extract
fresh fruit (strawberries, raspberries, sliced peaches etc.)
apricot jam or red-currant jelly, melted and strained, to glaze

Line tartlet pans with the pastry (use boat-shaped tins if you have them). Bake in a preheated oven at 375°F for about 10 minutes. When cold, brush the insides of the tartlet cases with the melted chocolate and leave to harden.

Mix together the cream cheese and heavy cream until very smooth, then add the sugar and vanilla extract. Fill the tartlet cases with the cream mixture and place fruit on top. Brush with apricot or red-currant glaze, depending on the fruit used, and leave to set.

JP

Maids of Honor

How singularly unapt is the name for these little medieval tarts. Henry VIII called them this after Anne Boleyn when she was lady in waiting to Catherine of Aragon. If Anne had only had a little more honor, or perhaps a little less, England might still be Catholic.

Makes 12

2 cups ricotta cheese
½ cup (1 stick) unsalted butter, softened
2 egg yolks
2 tablespoons brandy
2 tablespoons slivered almonds
1 teaspoon sugar
1 teaspoon ground cinnamon
grated zest and juice of ½ lemon
1 pound frozen puff pastry, thawed
currants to decorate

Press the ricotta and butter through a sieve. Beat the egg yolks briskly with the brandy and add to the cheese mixture. Add the almonds, sugar, cinnamon and lemon zest and juice.

Line 12 3-inch tartlet pans with the puff pastry. Fill with the cheese mixture and sprinkle with the currants. Bake in a preheated oven at 425°F for about 30 minutes or until well risen and golden brown.

CDW

Almond Pastry (The Snake)

I remember reading somewhere that this recipe originated in Morocco, and that the literal translation of its Moroccan name is "the snake". This might help to explain the coiling of the pastry. The almond paste mixture also makes delicious *petits fours*.

2¼ cups ground almonds
1½ cups confectioners' sugar, sifted, plus more for dusting
2–3 tablespoons orange flower water
½ teaspoon almond extract
1 egg white, beaten to stiff peaks
6 sheets of phyllo pastry
melted butter

Mix together the ground almonds, confectioners' sugar, orange flower water and almond extract to make a firm, dryish paste. Knead until smooth. Mix half the egg white into the paste; the remaining egg white will not be needed.

Divide the paste into three, and roll each piece into a long sausage about ¾-inch thick. Take a sheet of phyllo pastry and brush with melted butter. Cover with another sheet of phyllo and again brush with melted butter. Arrange a piece of almond paste lengthwise on the phyllo pastry and roll up carefully.

Have ready a greased loose-bottomed 8-inch tart pan. Carefully curl the pastry roll into a spiral in the pan, starting in the center. Make two more long sausage-shaped rolls, joining the second to the end of the first and the third to the end of the second and coiling round to the side of the pan. Brush "the snake" well with melted butter, then bake in a preheated oven at 350°F for 30 minutes or until golden brown. Cool in the pan on a wire rack. Remove from the pan and dust with confectioners' sugar when cool.

JP

Pikelets

Pikelet is a West Midland dialect term for a small flat crumpet. It comes from the Welsh "bara pyglyd," or pitchy bread — so typical and daft.

Makes 20–24

2 cups self-rising flour
1 teaspoon cream of tartar
½ teaspoon baking soda
3 tablespoons sugar
2 eggs
1¼ cups milk
4 tablespoons melted butter
bacon drippings or butter for frying

Sift the flour, cream of tartar, baking soda and sugar into a mixing bowl. Make a well in the center and break in the eggs. Combine the milk and melted butter and add gradually to the dry ingredients, mixing until you have smooth, lump-free batter.

Heat a griddle pan or a heavy frying pan. If you have some home-cured bacon, then a lump of fat on the end of a fork is ideal for greasing the griddle. Otherwise, use buttered parchment to wipe over the griddle. Pour little pools of the batter (about a large table-spoon each) on to the hot griddle and cook until you see tiny holes appearing on the top of the pikelets. Flip them over and carry on cooking until you think they are ready. Transfer the pikelets to a warm plate, cover with a paper towel to keep them warm and serve as soon as possible.

JP

Baklava

A popular dessert of the Eastern Mediterranean and Middle East. It seems to have appeared during the time of the Ottoman Empire, therefore its name is Turkish.

1½ cups chopped walnuts, or use hazelnuts, almonds, pistachio nuts or a mixture of nuts
⅓ cup sugar
1 teaspoon ground cinnamon
½ pound frozen phyllo pastry, thawed
6 tablespoons melted unsalted butter

FOR THE SYRUP:
⅔ cup sugar
⅔ cup water
1 tablespoon lemon juice
a good pinch of ground cinnamon
1 tablespoon rosewater or orange flower water

Mix the chopped walnuts with the sugar and cinnamon. Brush a baking pan (I use a jelly-roll pan) with melted butter and line it with four sheets of phyllo pastry, brushing each sheet with melted butter and cutting the sheets to fit the pan. Spread half the nut mixture over the pastry, then cover with two more sheets, each brushed with melted butter. Spread over the remaining nuts and cover with another four sheets of pastry, not forgetting to brush each with melted butter. Brush the top sheet with the remaining butter. Score the top in diamond shapes, using a sharp knife. Bake in a preheated oven at 350°F for 30–40 minutes or until golden brown, turning the oven up to 375°F for the last 10 minutes if the pastry needs browning.

While the baklava is baking make the syrup. Place the sugar, water and lemon juice in a small saucepan and warm over a low heat to dissolve the sugar. Bring to the boil and boil for 2 minutes. Add the cinnamon and rosewater or orange flower water. Pour the hot syrup over the baklava and leave to cool before cutting into the marked diamonds.

JP

Savory Shortcrust

I prefer to find something savory on a tea table — all cakes and jam can get rather sickly. These nice little morsels make a pleasant change.

Makes about 32

1 cup all-purpose flour
pinch of cayenne pepper
salt and freshly ground pepper
4 tablespoons (½ stick) butter
4 teaspoons Parmesan cheese,
freshly grated
1 egg yolk

FOR THE FILLING:
Dijon mustard
Gentleman's Relish (anchovy
paste)
1–2 tablespoons Parmesan
cheese, freshly grated
fresh chives, finely chopped

For the pastry, sift the flour, cayenne pepper and a seasoning of salt and pepper into a bowl. Rub in the butter, then add the grated cheese. Mix to a soft dough with the egg yolk, adding a few drops of water if necessary. Chill for 30 minutes.

Roll out the dough thinly into a square roughly 10 x 10 inches. Spread lightly with mustard, then cover the mustard with a thin film of Gentleman's Relish. Sprinkle over the Parmesan cheese and chives. Roll up as for a jelly roll, wrap in cling film and chill for 45 minutes.

Cut the roll across into thin slices and place on a greased and lined cooking sheet. Bake in a preheated oven at 375°F for 7–10 minutes.

JP

Queen Alexandra's Sandwiches

If only Princess Diana had taken this splendid woman for her role model, what a lean time the tabloids would have had. I am a great fan of this Queen who combined an impish sense of humor with enormous compassion. She sent for Mrs Keppell, Edward VII's favorite mistress (who was Camilla Parker Bowles' grandmother), to attend his death bed. This was her favorite sandwich recipe. Remember that it is an Edwardian sandwich, so cut the bread thin.

FOR THE MUSTARD BUTTER:
1½ cups (3 sticks) unsalted butter, at room temperature
1 tablespoon lemon juice
2 tablespoons mild French mustard

½ pound poached chicken, ground in a food processor
mayonnaise to bind
salt and freshly ground pepper
few drops of hot-pepper sauce
20 thin slices of brown bread
10 thin slices of roast lamb or boiled tongue
a bunch of watercress leaves

To make the mustard butter, beat all the ingredients together to a smooth paste. (Store in a jar in the refrigerator.)

Mix the chicken and mayonnaise with a fork, and season with salt, pepper and hot-pepper sauce. Spread half the slices of brown bread with the mustard butter. Lay slices of lamb or tongue on the bread and spread with the chicken mixture. Add watercress leaves. Top with the remaining slices of bread to make sandwiches, trim the crusts and cut into dainty squares.

CDW

Deviled Fish Sandwiches

These are also good for drinks parties.

½ pound any smoked fish
2 hard-cooked eggs, chopped
2 tablespoons chopped parsley
2 tablespoons chopped
fresh chives
2 tablespoons Worcestershire
sauce
several drops of hot-pepper
sauce
heavy cream to bind
salt and freshly ground pepper
thin slices of bread
softened butter

Mix together all the ingredients, except the bread and butter, to make a smooth paste. Butter the bread and spread half the slices with the filling. Make sandwiches, trim crusts, cut into squares and serve.

CDW

Scottish Seed Cake

This is my Aberdonian grandmother's recipe, and is more interesting than the English variety.

1 pound (4 sticks) butter, at room temperature
1 pound (2½ cups) sugar
9 eggs, beaten
1 pound (4 cups) all-purpose flour
½ teaspoon each ground cinnamon and grated nutmeg
¾ cup candied citron peel, chopped
⅓ cup each candied orange and lemon peel, chopped
¾ cup blanched almonds, chopped
1 ounce caraway comfits (caraway seeds set in hard caramel, broken into pieces)

Cream the butter and sugar together well. Beat in the eggs. Sift the flour and spices over the surface and fold into the mixture, together with the candied citrus peel and almonds. Sprinkle the top with the comfits. Turn into a greased and lined 10-inch cake pan. Bake in a preheated oven at 350°F for 2 hours.

CDW

Note: if you cannot get caraway comfits, use crushed nut brittle.

Illustrated overleaf

Gogo's Potted Meat

Gogo was the grandfather of my friend Carrotts, of flapjack fame (see page 122). Her son Nick, to whom she sent this potted meat when he was a student, is now a solicitor. He gave me my first-ever brief when I was a barrister, and once greatly delighted us by tying most of his clothes to the tail of a kite as it went ever higher into the stratosphere. I give the recipe to you as it was given to me. I think that it is the mace that gives it its cachet.

1½ pounds good beefsteak
2 whole cloves
¼ teaspoon ground mace
salt and freshly ground pepper
4 tablespoons (½ stick) butter
clarified butter

Cut up the beef in cubes, removing fat, skin and gristle. Put into a casserole, add the cloves, mace, salt and pepper, and cover with cold water. Place in a very low oven and stew very slowly for 2½–3 hours until tender. Strain the gravy into a basin, and pass the meat through a mincing machine three times or grind in a food processor. Reduce the gravy until it thickens and mix with the ground meat and butter, beating well to get a lovely smooth paste. Taste and add more seasoning if needed. (If you reduce the gravy too much and the potted meat is too stiff, you can always add a dash of hot water, or even a bit more butter to make it extra luscious.) Put into potted meat (small glass) jars and cover with clarified butter.

Note: I still use an old-fashioned mincing machine, but no doubt you bright young things have some bit of gadgetry that does the job rapidly and without effort. Mummy always said that to put meat through the mincer thrice was not only essential to get a smooth paste, but also had something to do with the Trinity – I suppose everything does, when you come to think of it.

CDW

Chocolate Brownies

I got this receipt years ago when I accompanied the sculptor Fiore de Henriquez on a lecture tour round the USA (top part). These are the classic brownies, much my most favorite cake in America, with its chewy texture and rich chocolate flavor. You could always throw in a handful of fresh dried cannabis to liven up a dull tea party – but beware the cops!

Makes about 30

4 ounces best bittersweet chocolate
½ cup (1 stick) butter
4 eggs
½ teaspoon salt
1 pound (2½ cups) sugar
1 teaspoon best vanilla extract
1 cup all-purpose flour
1 cup chopped pecans or walnuts
whipped cream (optional)

In a double-boiler or a bowl over a pan of barely simmering water, melt the chocolate and butter. Cool, then beat until foamy and light in color.

Beat the eggs, which should be at room temperature, with the salt, then gradually add the sugar and vanilla extract, beating all the time until really creamy.

Combine the cooled chocolate mixture with the eggs and sugar, with a few deft strokes, using a spatula, then fold in the sifted flour followed by the pecans or walnuts. Pour into a greased, 9 x 13-inch pan and bake in a preheated oven at 350°F for about 25 minutes, or until the center is just firm to the touch. Do not overcook.

Cool in the pan, then cut into squares. To store, wrap in aluminum foil. You can serve the brownies with whipped cream, or just chew them.

JP

COCKTAIL PARTIES

Move over Carmen Miranda, Jennifer shows how to shake things up
behind the bar at the Brazilian Embassy

CLARISSA WRITES: Jennifer reckons the cocktail party came over from America because the bright young things of the 1920s did not have the resources to face the interminable gap between the huge teas and even larger dinners of the post-First World War era. They needed constant entertainment lest they dwell on the horrors through which the world had just passed. Certainly the cocktail itself seems to have first flourished in the Prohibition period in America, as a disguise for bath-tub gin and other lethal concoctions, rather as designer drugs proliferate in today's underworld activities.

Jennifer, who goes to more cocktail parties than I do, says that the food veers from the old-fashioned soggy pastry and bits of bread with one prawn covered in gelatin to the greatly improved modern version where Oriental titbits and Levantine mezzes fill the gap much better. We owe a huge debt to Lorna Wing, whose brilliant ideas – miniaturised fish and chips in newspaper cones, and tiny Yorkshire puddings with roast beef and horseradish to name but two – did so much to make caterers rethink eats for drinks parties. Jennifer says that private drinks parties have now got out of hand: where the invitation stipulates 6–8pm, people arrive at nine and stay until eleven. In my younger day you had no option, as everyone went off to dinner half-an-hour after the allotted time was up.

For the filming of this programme our beloved director wanted an Embassy, and after much running about the Brazilians won the prize easily. They were much the most helpful and charming, and their Excellencies Ambassador and Señora Barbosa offered us the run of their lovely house, the use of their staff and even threw the party for us as if we had been the honored guests rather than a pesky television outfit. All we had to do was cook for it.

We have both spent a lot of our cooking careers dreaming up things to serve at cocktail parties, and as a bookseller I empathise with all those caterers who have to respond to their clients' demands for newer, wackier ideas. I hope this section will be of some help. If I have any advice at all, it is to have lots of a few delicious things, rather than a huge variety of choices. In Shakespeare's words, it is "vaulting ambition which o'erleaps itself." Good luck.

ABOVE *Clarissa prepares Acaraje for the Ambassador's party at the embassy*

RIGHT *A daring attempt at bike-stealing? Doorman Edward Whitcombe parks the motorcycle and sidecar outside the Dorchester*

Chicken Teriyaki

Do not overcook these as they tend to dry out and get tough (I'm sure you have often been offered these little bits of leather at drink parties).

1 pound boneless chicken breasts
2 ounces fresh ginger root, finely grated
2 tablespoons mirin (rice wine)
2 teaspoons sugar
2 tablespoons light soy sauce
2 tablespoons vegetable oil
2 tablespoons sake

Cut the chicken into bite-size pieces. Combine the grated ginger, mirin, sugar, soy sauce, vegetable oil and sake in a saucepan. Bring to the boil, then simmer gently for 15 minutes. Allow the mixture to cool. Marinate the chicken in this sauce for about 1 hour.

Thread the chicken pieces on to skewers. Cook under a preheated very hot broiler until cooked through, turning once and basting with the marinade when the chicken is turned over.

JP

Devils on Horseback

The chicken livers should still be very pink inside after sautéing, as they will cook again under the broiler. If overcooked they will be tough and grey.

chicken livers, trimmed
butter
cayenne pepper
ready-to-eat prunes, pitted
slices of bacon, cut in half

Gently sauté the chicken livers in a little butter, then cut into thin slices and dust lightly with cayenne pepper. Stuff the prunes with chicken livers. Stretch the bacon slices with a flat knife. Wrap a slice around each prune and secure with a wooden cocktail stick. Broil until the bacon is crisp, or bake in a preheated oven at 425°F for 5–6 minutes.

JP

Angels on Horseback

I have no idea where the "horseback" idiom came from. I see that devils are black and angels are white, but why on horseback? It sounds more like the Apocalypse.

fresh oysters
thin slices of bacon
salt and freshly ground pepper
small rounds of fried bread or toast
lemon juice
paprika

Wash and brush the grit from the oyster shells. Using a sharp, strong, pointed knife (a proper oyster knife if possible), insert the point of the blade into the hinge of the oyster. Slide along the hinge (this cuts the muscle), then twist to prise the shells apart. Your knife should be very sharp, so take great care. Remove the oysters from their shells, drain and remove the beard. Wrap each oyster in a slice of bacon and fasten with a wooden cocktail stick. Season with a sprinkling of salt and pepper. Broil just long enough to crisp the bacon, or bake in a preheated oven at 425°F for 5–6 minutes. Remove the stick and arrange each oyster on a round of fried or toasted bread. Sprinkle with a few drops of lemon juice. A dusting of paprika adds a little color.

JP

Prawns on Sugarcane Sticks

I don't know whether the poor unfortunates in the rest of the United Kingdom can buy sugarcane sticks, but in Edinburgh we can, as we are blessed with the best Mexican/South American deli this side of the pond. It is called Lupe Pintos and is owned by a splendid man named Duggie Bell, who is so wonderfully eccentric that for my first year in Edinburgh I thought "Lupe" was his nickname. If you can't get sugarcane sticks use wooden saté sticks, but don't forget to soak them first.

Makes 16

olive oil
a 2-inch piece of fresh root
ginger, chopped
2 garlic cloves, chopped
2 whole scallions, chopped
1 hot chile, chopped
soy sauce
juice of 2 limes
16 raw tiger or king prawns
(jumbo shrimp) in the shell
4 sugarcane sticks

In a heavy pan heat a little oil and fry the ginger, garlic, scallions and chile. Add a dash of soy sauce and the lime juice. Transfer this mixture to a bowl. Add the prawns, turn to coat and leave to marinate overnight.

Thread the prawns on to the sugarcane sticks. Place under a pre-heated broiler and cook for 3–4 minutes on each side, painting with more marinade once or twice. They can also be cooked on the grill. The sugarcane sticks add a wonderful flavor.

CDW

Broiled Mussels

These make a welcome change in the cocktail stakes.

4 pints mussels
6 tablespoons white
bread crumbs
4 tablespoons chopped
parsley
2 garlic cloves, finely chopped
2 tablespoons chopped fresh
chives
⅔ cup olive oil
salt and freshly ground pepper

Wash and scrape the mussels thoroughly under cold running water and remove the beards. Put the mussels in a pan, without any water, and heat until the shells open. (Any that remain unopened must be discarded.) Discard the empty shells, and loosen the mussels from the other shells. Arrange the mussels, in the bottom shell halves, in a cooking tray. Mix together the bread crumbs, parsley, garlic, chives, olive oil, salt and pepper. Spoon the mixture over each mussel and leave for about half an hour before cooking.

Put the mussels under a preheated broiler for just a few minutes to brown the crumb mixture and form a crust over the mussels. Try not to overcook.

JP

Oysters Rockefeller

Unless you are adept at opening oysters, I should get help from an expert. Otherwise your hands might be like Lady Macbeth imagined hers to be. If you want to open the oysters yourself, see the recipe for Angels on Horseback (page 141) for instructions.

Makes 24

24 fresh oysters, opened and left on the half shell
rock salt
4 tablespoons olive oil
½ cup (1 stick) butter
3 tablespoons chopped parsley
2 tablespoons chopped celery
2 tablespoons chopped shallots
1 garlic clove, finely chopped
6 tablespoons chopped watercress
2 tablespoons chopped fennel
3 tablespoons white bread crumbs
2½ tablespoons Pernod
salt and freshly ground pepper

Loosen the oysters in their bottom shell halves, then arrange them on a bed of rock salt on two cooking trays (or use crumpled aluminum foil instead of rock salt).

Heat the olive oil and butter in a frying pan, wait for them to sizzle and then add the parsley, celery, shallots and garlic. Cook for 2–3 minutes. Add the watercress and fennel and cook for another minute, then add the bread crumbs, Pernod, salt and pepper. Purée the sauce in a blender or food processor.

Put a tablespoon of the sauce over each oyster in its shell. Bake in a preheated oven at 425°F for 4–5 minutes.

JP

Beignets au Fromage

These are heavenly mouthfuls. Think of them as hot cheesy profiteroles, but much better.

½ cup plus 2 tablespoons all-purpose flour
pinch of dry English mustard powder
salt and freshly ground pepper
3 tablespoons (⅜ stick) butter
½ cup water
2 eggs, beaten
1 cup grated Gruyère or Parmesan cheese (or you could mix the two cheeses)
oil for deep frying
paprika

Sift the flour and mustard on to a sheet of parchment and add a seasoning of salt and pepper. Heat the butter and water in a heavy saucepan and bring to the boil. Remove from the heat, add the sifted ingredients to the pan and mix well. Return to the heat and beat until the paste is smooth and pulls away from the sides of the pan. Remove from the heat again and leave the mixture to cool slightly. Gradually add the eggs, beating thoroughly. Add the cheese and mix in.

Heat oil for deep frying until it is hot enough to brown a cube of bread in 60 seconds. Taking a heaping teaspoonful of the paste for each beignet, drop them into the hot oil and fry for 7–10 minutes or until golden brown all over and doubled in size. Don't put too many beignets in at the same time: they should not be crowded as they fry. Drain well on paper towels and serve immediately, sprinkled with paprika.

JP

Gambas en Gabardinas

My mother had a Spanish couple who worked for her as cook and butler. At parties he would play the guitar and she would sing. She was very fiery – one day my mother suggested they watch a rather good production of *Carmen* on their television, and Isabella nearly stabbed Carlos in a fit of jealous rage because she remembered he had flirted with a gypsy twenty years before! I was fascinated by the name of this dish, which means prawns in mackintoshes. I am grateful to Pepita Aris, whose writings I love, for giving the true recipe in her splendid book, *Recipes from a Spanish Village*. With the inaccuracy of childhood memory I had developed a different version, which I also give here.

Makes about 20

PEPITA'S VERSION

1 pound raw king or tiger prawns (jumbo shrimp) in the shell
oil for deep frying

FOR THE BATTER:

1 cup all-purpose flour
pinch of salt
3 tablespoons melted butter
pinch of cayenne pepper
¾ cup warm water (105° to 115°F)
1 egg white
lemon wedges

MY VERSION

1 pound phyllo pastry or Chinese spring roll skins, thawed if frozen
melted butter
jar of jalapeño paste
20 raw king or tiger prawns (jumbo shrimp), peeled
salt and freshly ground pepper

Make the batter by mixing together all the ingredients, except the egg white, until smooth, then leave to stand.

Peel the prawns, leaving on the tip of the tail. Heat oil to the top heat on an electric deep fat fryer, or until the oil is hot enough to crisp a bread cube in 35 seconds. Whisk the egg white and fold into the batter. Holding each prawn by the tail, dip it into the batter and then lower into the hot oil. Let it fry for 30 seconds or until puffed up and golden brown all over. Remove and drain on kitchen paper. Serve at once, with lemon wedges.

Remember that phyllo pastry becomes brittle if it is allowed to dry out, so as soon as you unwrap it cover it with a damp kitchen towel. Take a pastry sheet and brush with melted butter. Cut each sheet into quarters. Place a small dollop of jalapeño paste on each quarter-sheet, top with a prawn and season with salt and pepper. Roll the prawn up in the pastry. Place the prawn parcel, seam side down, on a lightly greased cooking sheet. When all the parcels have been prepared, bake in a preheated oven at 400°F for about 20 minutes or until golden brown.

CDW

Bolinhos de Bacalhau (Portuguese Cod Cakes)

The receipt for these delicious fish balls was taught to me in Portugal by Jonnie Cobb. He always said that even the true Portuguese Brit, who normally shuddered at the thought of *bacalhau*, never hesitates to make a complete beast of himself at the sight of these crispy delicacies.

10 ounces thick salt cod
½ pound floury potatoes
butter and milk for the potatoes
3 heaping tablespoons finely chopped parsley
1 heaping tablespoon finely chopped fresh mint
freshly ground black pepper
3 eggs, separated
1 tablespoon port (optional)
oil for deep frying

A day or two before you are making the fish cakes, put the cod to soak in cold water for 24–36 hours. Change the water four or five times during this time.

Drain the cod and rinse it well under cold running water. Cover with fresh water in a saucepan, bring to the boil and simmer for about 20 minutes or until the cod is soft. While the cod is simmering, cook the potatoes in their skins, then peel and mash them with a little butter and milk, to a fairly stiff consistency. When the cod is ready, drain it thoroughly and remove the skin and bones. Shred the cod with a couple of forks. Add the creamed potatoes, parsley, mint, black pepper and egg yolks, and the port, if using. Mix thoroughly. Whisk the egg whites until stiff, then fold into the cod mixture. Take a lump of the mixture, about the size of a small egg, and mould it in your hand to make a torpedo shape. Deep fry in very hot oil until crisp and brown all over. Drain on paper towels and serve hot.

JP

Cheese Soufflé Tartlets

These little creatures, taken from Margaret Costa's *Four Seasons Cookery Book*, should be served immediately, or at least still hot, or they lose their charm.

Makes about 24

FOR THE PASTRY SHELLS:
2 cups self-rising flour
4 tablespoons lard
4 tablespoons (½ stick) butter

FOR THE SOUFFLÉ FILLING:
4 ounces bacon, finely chopped
1 medium onion, finely chopped
2 tablespoons (¼ stick) butter, melted
¼ cup all-purpose flour
⅔ cup milk
salt and pepper
2 eggs, separated
1 cup grated cheese

To make the pastry shells, sift the flour into a bowl and rub in the lard and butter. Press into a dough, gradually adding iced water to bind. Use to line 2¼-inch tartlet pans.

Fry the bacon gently in its own fat. Add the onion and fry gently until soft. Set aside.

To make a white sauce, melt the butter over a low heat, add the flour and cook over the low heat for a minute or two, stirring all the time. Gradually add the milk to the flour and butter roux, stirring constantly, over the low heat. Cook the sauce for about 3 minutes, then season well. Allow the mixture to cool slightly before beating in the egg yolks and grated cheese. Whisk the egg whites until stiff and fold into the cheese mixture. Divide the bacon and onion mixture among the pastry shells. Cover each with a spoonful of the soufflé mixture. Bake in a preheated oven at 400°F for about 20 minutes, until golden brown.

JP

Illustrated overleaf

Acaraje

I had my first ever food experience in Brazil, aged five. When I returned to school, the nuns enquired what I had liked best – the humming birds?, the Christ of the Andes? My reply was: the black beans, braised beef and rice. I have since visited South America several times, but my stomach still gladdens most at the thought of Brazil.

These little bean fritters with dried prawns are a traditional dish, very moreish and good for parties. If you can get it, the oil for frying should be one-quarter *dende* oil for the right flavor. This is palm oil and can be bought in Afro Caribbean grocers. I serve the fritters with a hot sauce.

Makes 20

1 pound dried black eyed peas
1 onion, roughly chopped
1 maleguata chile pepper or use ½ teaspoon hot-pepper sauce
salt and freshly ground pepper
oil for deep frying
20 small dried prawns (these can be bought in Asian grocers)

Soak the black-eyed peas overnight in cold water, changing the water once. Then rub the peas between the palms of your hands to free the outer skins, which should float to the surface. Scoop off the skins and discard. Drain the peas. Purée the peas and onion in a food processor. Season with the chile or hot-pepper sauce, salt and pepper. Using two soup spoons, form the pea mixture into small egg shapes. Press a dried prawn into the center of each one, and press the bean mixture round to secure it. The prawn should still stand proud. Heat the oil to 350°F, and fry the fritters in small batches until golden brown all over. Remove with a slotted spoon and drain on paper towels. Keep warm in a warm oven until they are all fried.

CDW

Aberdeen Nips

My grandmother, who was from Aberdeen, firmly believed that one could never have enough smoked haddock. This little dish is an excellent way of using up left-over cooked smoked haddock and is brilliant for drinks parties or for high tea.

Makes 32 pieces

12 ounces cooked smoked
haddock
4 egg yolks
1¼ cups thick white sauce
salt and freshly ground pepper
cayenne pepper
8 slices of buttered toast,
crusts removed, each cut into
quarters
paprika

Flake the fish finely. Mix the fish and the egg yolks into the sauce and season with salt, pepper and cayenne pepper. Heat the mixture through gently in a saucepan over a low heat. Pile on the squares of buttered toast, sprinkle with paprika and serve.

CDW

Kipper Rarebit

Our beloved director, Patricia Llewellyn, is, as you might guess, Welsh, and I have in the last year been more kindly disposed towards the Welsh than ever before. So when I decided to resolve to my own satisfaction the rabbit/rarebit debate that has been raging since the eighteenth century, I turned to Welsh history for guidance. The Welsh have always had a passion for cheese, and *caws pobi*, or cheese rabbit, was credited to them in the fourteenth century. Rarebit, meaning soft, seems to come on the scene much later. This dish is, of course, post-1865, as kippers didn't exist before that date.

Makes 32 pieces

2 pairs of kippers
2½ cups milk
2 garlic cloves, crushed
4 tablespoons (½ stick) butter
½ cup all-purpose flour
1 cup grated strong Cheddar
or *Penty Bont* cheese
2 hard-cooked eggs, chopped
paprika
8 slices of fried bread or toast,
crusts removed, each cut into
quarters

Put the kippers in the milk and bring to the boil, then remove from the heat and leave to stand for 5 minutes. Remove the kippers, and take the flesh from the skin and bones. Return the skin and bones to the milk, add the garlic and simmer for 10 minutes; strain. Make a white sauce with the milk, butter and flour according to the procedure on page 149. Fold in the cheese and the flaked kipper flesh. Heat through, then add the eggs and paprika to taste. Serve on the fried bread or toast.

CDW

Romanoff Savory

The Romanoffs would consider this dish very plebian, but in fact it is quite interesting.

Serves 6–12

6 hard-cooked eggs, chopped
3 tablespoons mayonnaise
1 medium onion, very finely chopped
1 cup plus 2 tablespoons cream cheese
plain yogurt
4 ounces caviar
lemon wedges and parsley sprigs to garnish
crackers or melba toast

Combine the hard-cooked eggs and mayonnaise, and spread over the bottom of a well-greased 8-inch loose-bottomed cake pan. Scatter over the onion. Soften the cream cheese by blending it with the yogurt, then spread it over the onion using a wet spatula. Cover and chill for at least 3 hours or overnight.

Before serving, top with the caviar, and garnish with lemon wedges and parsley sprigs. Serve with crackers or melba toast.

JP

Bagna Caóda

This is essentially a hot dip for raw vegetables. Use carrots, celery, cauliflower florets, fennel, bell peppers, radishes, scallions and zucchini, (preferably partly cooked). The dip is ready when the ingredients are well blended and smooth. If there is any left over, break some eggs into it and scramble the resulting mixture.

½ cup (1 stick) butter
2 tablespoons olive oil
4 garlic cloves, finely chopped
1½ cans anchovy fillets, drained

Heat the butter and oil very gently in an earthenware pot (if you have one), or a saucepan, and add the finely chopped garlic. Pound the anchovies into a paste, then add to the pot and stir. Keep the dip warm all the time it is being used in the same way as a fondue, over a spirit lamp in the middle of the table.

JP

Oat Cakes

It is very easy to make oat cakes, and they are much better than any you can buy. The recipe I use is from Lady Clarke of Tillypronie, whose book I love and rely on a lot, as did the late Elizabeth David whose copy I now own. Lady Clarke went round collecting recipes, and this one is noted as from J. Emslie 1893. I quote the recipe verbatim, with the one suggestion that unless you have an open fire you should finish the cakes off under a slow broiler.

(see method for ingredients)

Make a dough from 1⅔ cups fine oatmeal, freshly ground and kept from the air, a pinch of salt, ½ teaspoon baking powder and as little cream as possible – only just enough to make it a dough. Too thick cream does not do. Roll it out as thin as possible and cut into three cornered pieces. Put it on the girdle [griddle to you] to set. It must not be turned over or it will be tough, but put it on the toaster in front of the fire to brown the top side, toaster sloping towards fire. If baked in an oven an oat cake will be hard.

I like to serve oat cakes topped with *carpaccio* of venison, which I buy from Nicholas Fletcher at Auchtermuchty by post. You can make this yourself by freezing raw venison, slicing it very thin and marinating it in olive oil and herbs for 24 hours.

CDW

Blinys

Oh how I love blinys (which are also spelled blinis). When I was a child we had some Russian friends who used to eat them in huge quantities throughout the week before Lent. When we would go to their house, there would be these delicious little pancakes which you could heap with sour cream and caviar, or with cod's roe mixed with cream cheese, crisp bacon fried with scallions, herrings of all types, chopped liver, smoked sturgeon and all manner of other good things. The Russians also eat them with fruit purée or jam, but I am a savory bliny addict.
The pancakes are yeasted and made with a mixture of plain flour and buckwheat flour, which gives them a nutty flavor and more texture than an ordinary pancake. My friend Isobel Rutherford has a set of tiny cast-iron bliny pans which I greatly covet, but you can make them successfully in an ordinary small frying pan.

½ ounce fresh yeast or a
¼ ounce envelope active
dry yeast
1¼ cups milk, warmed
2 large eggs, separated
⅔ cup sour cream
1 teaspoon salt
1 cup white bread flour
1 cup buckwheat flour
oil for frying

Cream the yeast with a little of the milk, then add the remaining milk, the egg yolks and sour cream. (If you are using ordinary dry yeast, mix it with a little cold water and leave it for 10 minutes before using; easy-blend dried yeast can be added to the flour.) Sift the flour and salt into a bowl and add the yeast mixture. Stir to make a thick batter. Leave for at least an hour in a warm place, or overnight if more convenient. The batter should now look bubbly. Stir it well. Just before cooking, whisk the egg whites until stiff and fold them into the batter.

Heat a little oil in your pan and pour off any excess. Then pour in a tablespoon of the batter. Turn the pancake over when it shows bubbles on the top side. Cook lots – one bliny is never enough!

CDW

Pumpernickel

Pumpernickel makes a great base for party canapés because it has a flavor of its own that enhances fairly strong toppings, and it doesn't go soggy. Although it is the cheapest form of bread in Germany, it is a luxury item in Britain. I must confess I find something exotic and romantic about it. It is easy to make.

½ cup (1 stick) butter
¾ cup brown sugar, packed
1 teaspoon ground cinnamon
3 eggs
1 pound rye flour
½ teaspoon baking powder
½ cup shelled hazelnuts, finely chopped

In a food processor cream the butter with the sugar and cinnamon. Add the eggs, one by one, and process until very smooth. Add the flour, baking powder and nuts, and mix in. If dough is too dry add a little water. Roll out to ¼-inch thick and transfer to a lightly greased cooking sheet. Bake in a preheated oven at 325°F for 25 minutes. Cut into desired shapes immediately on removing from the oven. Cool the shapes separately on a wire rack.

Good toppings for pumpernickel include any form of pickled herring, Old Man's Mess (see page 32), eye of the egg, very spicy steak tartare, cucumber in sour cream, or blue cheese and celery.

CDW

Sushi

Sushi requires a deft hand. In fact, real sushi makers are trained for years, but you can master a resemblance of the real thing after a few tries. You will need a bamboo sushi mat for these.

1 pound plus 1 ounce sushi rice (short-grain pudding rice is not a suitable alternative)
1 tablespoon sugar
4½ tablespoons rice vinegar or, if unavailable, cider vinegar may be used
1 heaping teaspoon salt
5 sheets of nori (toasted paper-thin sheets of laver seaweed)

SUGGESTED FILLINGS:
tuna, very fresh or canned, and shredded lettuce
pickled herring and shredded lettuce
crab sticks with cress
asparagus and mayonnaise
very thin omelet strips with cress
cucumber sticks with cress
avocado with cress and mayonnaise (although not authentic, this is delicious and very popular)

Put the rice in a large saucepan with 2½ cups of cold water and allow to stand for 30 minutes. Bring contents of saucepan to the boil and allow to boil rapidly for 1 minute, then cover saucepan tightly and simmer contents for 20 minutes. Remove from the heat and allow to stand for a further 10 minutes without removing the lid.

In the meantime, dissolve the sugar in the rice vinegar. Add the salt. Turn the rice into a large bowl and sprinkle over the vinegar mixture to cool the rice quickly and make it shiny.

To make the sushi rolls, place your sushi mat on the table in front of you and put a sheet of nori on top, positioning it about ½ inch above the bottom of the mat. Put a thin layer of vinegared rice over the bottom two thirds of the sheet of nori, making sure you spread the rice to the edges. Dipping your spatula in a tumbler of rice vinegar mixed with water will help to spread the rice and prevent stickiness. Place your chosen filling in a thin layer on the rice, just below the center. Then, pinching the mat and the nori between your fingers at the outer edges, roll the mat over the rice and press gently with your hands. Let the mat fall back, and roll the nori over completely like a jelly roll. Press again lightly with your hands. Place the roll on a plate while you continue to make further rolls. The rolls should be allowed to rest for 2–3 minutes before cutting across into pieces about ½ inch thick (use a sharp knife dipped frequently into the vinegar and water mixture to prevent sticking).

If liked, serve sushi with a dipping sauce made from soy sauce mixed with a tiny blob of wasabi (Japanese horseradish) paste.

JP

161

Caipirinha

This receipt was given to me by Joseph, the chauffeur at the Brazilian Embassy. He made this on the program. It tastes so fresh you might think it is just a charming drink, but beware. It's a killer!

7 limes
a 70 cl bottle of aguardente or cachaça
superfine sugar
lots of crushed ice

Cut the limes in half and squash them with a piece of wood or your hand, as much as you can, to get all the juice out. Strain the juice through a sieve into a jug. Pour in the aguardente or cachaça. Sweeten with sugar according to your taste. (Taste several times!) Mix with a wooden spoon. When all the sugar has dissolved, add lots of ice. If the drink is too strong then add more ice. Serve in a small glass with a cube of ice.

JP

Royal Bombay Yacht Club Cocktail

As drunk by the very drunk at the Royal Bombay yacht club, to get drunker!

Serves 1

1½ jiggers brandy
2 dashes angostura bitters
1 teaspoon each pineapple syrup, maraschino and orange curaçao
a small strip of lime peel

Pour all the ingredients into a cocktail shaker, filled with crushed ice and shake. Strain into a cocktail glass and add a twist of lime peel.

CDW

Bengal Lancers' Punch

How dashing they looked in their uniforms, this splendid cavalry regiment. This was their regimental punch for special occasions.

Serves 20

½ cup each freshly squeezed orange juice, lime juice and pineapple juice
¼ cup superfine sugar
¾ cup each rum and Cointreau
2 bottles of red Bordeaux-type wine
1 bottle of Champagne
2 cups soda water

Combine the juices and sugar in a bowl and stir well. Add the rum, Cointreau and red wine. Place a block of ice in the bowl, and pour on the Champagne and soda water. Serve.

CDW

PICNICS

The "Black Prince" comes fully equipped for picnics, with its own sturdy wicker basket

CLARISSA WRITES: Jennifer comes from a picnicking background and her much-traveled life has led to alfresco eating in many glamorous spots. She tells one wonderful story of a picnic in Portugal where they all set off (some of the most doubting carrying sandwiches) and when they arrived at their destination they discovered their host's servants had brought tables and chairs, silver and napery, to say nothing of the delicious food, to a secluded spot. Frittata with the fishermen at Taormina in Sicily, diving for sea urchins to eat straight from the rocks, pig-sticking outings with the Hussars in Benghazi and wontons by the Yangtze in China are just a few of her many other picnic experiences. Catherine the Great of Russia had a picnic hamper with gold accoutrements which took eight footmen to lift – I could see that suiting Jennifer, although I would insist on selecting the footmen!

I am the baby in my lot and all the family activities had palled by the time I was old enough to enjoy them. It was usually a case of the Lido at Venice or the Ritz at Madrid for our holidays, but we did manage a few good picnics. My first memory is of a picnic in the woods at Ripley, near the Royal Horticultural Society at Wisley, the taste of a good cold sausage and the joy of peeling a hard-cooked egg cleanly; then there were picnics at point-to-points, sitting on damp rugs eating delicious home-made pies and pasties. I remember a wonderful picnic I took to Royal Ascot with lobster, asparagus and Champagne, and of course seaside picnics with the sand getting in the Marmite sandwiches. However I am not, I think, a picnic person; picnics seem to me to involve carting a lot of food large distances to eat in circumstances and temperatures less pleasant than if one had stayed at home. The best picnic I ever went to was organised by that great cook Alaphia Bidwell. She took all her friends on a narrowboat down the Thames and upon arrival at a suitable, but not preselected spot, trestles were unloaded and a fantastic meal was served. After a lavish, three-hour feast, we had to hurry back to catch the locks before they closed for the night.

I have, in middle age, acquired a taste for camping and love cooking on my primus stove, although I tend to go for food of the fillet and foie gras variety. For the program we have chosen a seaside picnic. I think our beloved director has dreams of donkey rides and golden sands. I hate to cast nasturtiums, as they say, but I shall keep my thermals and my Barbour jacket handy.

TOP *The final conquest: production researcher Steven Surbey joins Jennifer and Clarissa on the Devil's Bridge at Kirkby Lonsdale, Cumbria*

RIGHT *At the end of a long day's filming, Clarissa and Jennifer relax in the shade*

Ham Cake

This is a dish from Durham, which I imagine was originally taken to the pits as a daily piece by the local miners. It is made with cold left-over picnic ham, which I love, and scone mix.

1 pound all-purpose flour
1 teaspoon baking powder
1 cup (2 sticks) lard or butter
1 pound boiled ham, sliced

Sift the flour and baking powder into a bowl and rub in the lard or butter to a soft crumb texture. Add enough cold water to bind to a dough. Cut the dough in half and roll out into two rounds, each 7-inches diameter. Put the sliced ham on one round, cover with the other and press down to release any trapped air. Pinch the edges together to seal and prick all over with a fork. Bake in a pre-heated oven at 400°F for 25–30 minutes or until golden brown.

CDW

Tartine from Provence

This is a very good type of sandwich to take on picnics, being easy to handle, full of flavor, moist, succulent and even healthy. The bread is very important, so do try to get very good baguettes made with French flour or the best you can find from a good bakery.

1 long baguette or 4 little ones, halved
garlic cloves, halved
12 fine black olives, pitted
1 red bell pepper, sliced
some cooked French beans
2 large tomatoes, chopped
4 anchovy fillets
2 tablespoons delicious olive oil
1 teaspoon lemon juice or wine vinegar
salt and freshly ground pepper

Cut the bread in half lengthwise and rub the cut surfaces with garlic. In a food processor, or with a mortar and pestle and some elbow grease, mash together the olives, red bell pepper, beans, chopped tomatoes and anchovies. Mix in the olive oil and lemon juice or vinegar. Adjust seasoning with salt, if necessary, and pepper. Spread the mixture thickly over the bread and put the sides back together again. Tie up with string and enclose in aluminum foil or greaseproof paper. Place a board on top of the parcel with a few weights on it and press for about an hour. Then off you go to your picnic.

JP

Tortilla

This rustic, filling omelet from Spain is easy to eat when cut into wedges. I usually prefer the Italian fritatta, another flat omelet, but this is a welcome alternative. Make sure the potatoes are the waxy variety.

4 tablespoons olive oil
1 large onion, finely sliced
2 garlic cloves, finely sliced
1 pound potatoes, peeled and diced
salt and freshly ground pepper
6 eggs, beaten

Heat the oil in a large, heavy non-stick frying pan and add the onion and garlic. Stir round for a few minutes, then add the potatoes. Season with salt and pepper. Cook very slowly until the potatoes are tender, stirring occasionally but being careful not to break them up. When the potatoes and onions are cooked, remove them carefully with a slotted spoon to remove as much oil as possible before adding to the eggs. Pour off excess oil from the pan, just leaving a thin film of oil. Season the egg mixture a little. Reheat the pan, return the potatoes and onions to it, add the egg mixture and cook until the omelet is golden brown on the base. Cover the frying pan with a large plate and invert the frying pan, so the omelet falls on to the plate cooked side uppermost. Slide the omelet back into the pan and fry until the bottom side is golden brown. Alternatively, if you do not wish to turn the omelet over in the frying pan, finish it off under the broiler.

JP

Glazed Chicken Wings

Chicken wings are just about the cheapest things you can buy, and yet they have more flavor than the rest of the chicken. Prepared this way they are ideal for picnics — nice and sticky.

2½ tablespoons soy sauce
4 medium garlic cloves, minced
1 tablespoon Chinese chile oil
5 tablespoons honey
2½ tablespoons orange juice
2½ tablespoons cider vinegar
5 level tablespoons Dijon mustard
16 chicken wings

Mix all the ingredients, except the chicken wings, in a large bowl. Remove and discard the tips from the chicken wings. Place the wings in the bowl and turn to coat with the mixture. Leave to marinate in a cool place for at least 30 minutes, or for a couple of hours if possible.

Remove the wings from the marinade, place on a cooking sheet and cook in a preheated oven at 400°F for 25–30 minutes, or until cooked through. Baste once or twice with the marinade during cooking. Finish off under a hot broiler, for not more than 5 minutes.

JP

Deviled Pheasant Legs

In my pheasant farming days I came to understand the story of the small boy who, when arriving late at his prep school and asked, "Do you want anything to eat?", replied, "Oh nothing difficult, just a little cold pheasant." When you have pheasants you are endlessly looking for ways to prepare them. You wake in the night dreaming of pheasant and rosehips or something equally bizarre. This is really a breakfast dish, but in this day and age it is more successful for picnics. It can also be done with chicken or guinea fowl.

When you are dressing your pheasant you must pull the sinews from the leg. Snap the bone just above the foot and twist it round and round, then put it over a weight-bearing object and pull; the foot will come away, pulling all the sinews from the leg with it. Your butcher or game dealer will do this for you if asked; however, supermarkets merely cut the foot off so that you cannot pull out the sinews. Nor can you tell how old your bird is.

8 pheasant legs
2 tablespoons Worcestershire sauce
1 tablespoon olive oil
2 teaspoons dry English mustard powder
1 teaspoon cayenne pepper
salt and freshly ground pepper

Make deep diagonal slashes in the pheasant legs all the way round. Mix together the remaining ingredients and rub into the slashes. Leave the legs to sit for half an hour, then broil slowly or roast in a preheated oven at 350°F for 10–15 minutes or until cooked. Serve hot or cold.

CDW

Jambon Persillé

If taking this beautiful dish on a picnic, it is advisable to keep it chilled in an insulated container.

a 3-pound piece of boneless
uncooked ham
1 ham knuckle bone
1 pig's trotter
1 bottle of dry white wine
few sprigs of fresh tarragon
few sprigs of fresh chervil
few sprigs of fresh thyme
2 bay leaves
1 teaspoon peppercorns
a wine glass (4–5fl oz) of
tarragon vinegar
salt
5 tablespoons chopped parsley

Blanch the ham by placing in a large saucepan, covering with cold water and bringing to the boil. Simmer for 5 minutes and drain. Remove the skin. Cut the ham into large pieces. Return to the pan and add the ham bone, pig's trotter and white wine. Add a little water if necessary to ensure that the ham is covered. Add the tarragon, chervil, thyme, bay leaves and peppercorns. Bring to the boil, then simmer for about 2 hours or until the ham is very tender.

Remove the ham and strain the stock, discarding the trotter, ham bone and herbs. Flake the ham with a fork and place in a large glass bowl. When the stock has cooled, remove the fat. Add the tarragon vinegar and check the seasoning. When the stock begins to coagulate stir in the parsley, and pour over the ham. Leave to set in a cold place. Serve either direct from the bowl or turned out on to a plate.

JP

Mitton of Pork

This is a Northumbrian dish, and much as I try to attribute it to the great huntsman Squire Mitton, I have singularly failed to find any reason to do so. This dish can be served hot and is very good with mushrooms, but I like it best as a cold dish to take on a picnic. The secret of its success lies in the stuffing which needs to be fresh, interesting and well-flavored.

½ pound slices of bacon
1½ pounds pork tenderloin, thinly sliced
6 ounces sage and onion stuffing (not from a packet)
salt and freshly ground pepper
½ teaspoon ground mace

Line a 7-inch diameter pudding basin with most of the bacon slices, reserving a few for the top. Put in a layer of pork, then a layer of stuffing, and season with salt, pepper and mace. Continue this layering process until the basin is full, finishing with the reserved bacon. Press down well, then cover closely. Stand the basin in a baking pan to catch any drips. Bake in a preheated oven at 350°F for 1 hour. Place a weighted board over the pudding and leave until completely cold. To serve, turn the mitton out and slice.

CDW

Spare Ribs

If you want the rib meat to be really tender you can pre-boil the ribs for 20 minutes before putting them in the marinade. It makes eating them easier, although they are nice messy things to gnaw in the fingers. Take a damp cloth to wipe your hands.

2 tablespoons oil
3 tablespoons clear honey
½-inch piece of fresh ginger root, finely chopped
2 tablespoons dark soy sauce
2 tablespoons hoisin sauce
1 teaspoon five spice powder
2 garlic cloves, crushed
2 pounds spare ribs

Combine all the ingredients, except the spare ribs, in a jug and mix well. Pour over the ribs and leave to marinate for as long as possible, ideally overnight. Place the ribs on a rack in a roasting pan. Cook in a preheated oven at 400°F for about 45 minutes, turning the ribs over half way through the cooking time. Allow to cool and serve cold.

JP

Kibbeh

If the kibbeh can be kept slightly warm, so much the better. They are very good morsels either warm or cool, but better not chilled. Making the oval shapes is difficult at first, although practise makes perfect. Until the art is mastered it may be as well to make the kibbeh in a tray and to bake them. I give both methods here.

FOR THE SHELL:
1 cup bulghur wheat
1 pound ground lamb
1 small onion, finely chopped
salt and freshly ground black pepper
½ teaspoon ground cinnamon
oil for deep frying

FOR FILLING:
1 large onion, chopped
2 tablespoons oil
½ pound ground lamb
3 ounces pine nuts
½ teaspoon ground allspice
salt and freshly ground black pepper

To make the shell, put the bulghur wheat in a large bowl and cover with cold water. Swirl round with your fingers, then drain in a sieve. Squeeze out excess moisture, a handful at a time, and transfer to a clean bowl. Add the lamb, onion, salt, pepper and cinnamon to the bulghur. Work, in batches, in a food processor to reduce to a very soft and smooth texture. A little cold water may be added to help achieve this.

The filling is much coarser-textured than the shell. Sauté the onion in the oil until golden and soft, then add the lamb and fry until browned and crumbly. Add pine nuts, allspice, salt and pepper.

To make the kibbeh in the traditional way, take a small lump (about the size of an egg) of the shell mixture and shape into a ball. Make a hole in the center, and try to form the ball into a long, thin oval shape. Put a small teaspoon of the filling into the hole and close the shell by wetting with cold water and sticking the edges together. (A bowl of cold water is handy to moisten the hands.) Deep fry the kibbeh, in batches, in hot oil until a deep golden brown all over. Drain on paper towels.

The easier method is to smooth half the shell mixture over the base of a buttered baking pan, spread the filling over evenly and then cover with the remaining shell mixture. Cut into triangles. Melt ½ cup (1 stick) of butter and pour over the kibbeh. Bake in a preheated oven at 350°F for 45 minutes to 1 hour or until golden brown.

JP

Mantega Colorada

This is the Spanish version of pork rillettes, and I much prefer it to the French dish because it has a good color, as the name suggests, and is much tastier. Once we changed to a Spanish cook we always had it on picnics.

1 pound pork back fat, skin removed
1 pound belly of pork
4 garlic cloves, peeled
a wine glass (4–5fl oz) of dry sherry
2 bay leaves
2 tablespoons paprika
1–2 teaspoons freshly grated nutmeg
salt and freshly ground pepper

Cut the fat into the smallest possible cubes, and cut the belly into strips following the grain of the meat. Put the fat and belly pork into a casserole with the garlic cloves, sherry, bay leaves, paprika, nutmeg, salt and pepper. Cook in a preheated oven at 275°F for 6 hours, stirring occasionally.

Turn into a colander set over a bowl. Press down on the meat with the back of a spoon to drain it well. Pick the meat into shreds with a fork, then add to the fat in the bowl and stir to mix. Taste for seasoning. Keep in the refrigerator until needed.

CDW

Duck Terrine

Take some good bread and butter along with you to eat this on.

Serves 6-8

a 4–4½ pound duck, with its liver, cut up
1 pound belly of pork
1 chicken liver
4 tablespoons port
4 tablespoons red wine
10 juniper berries, crushed
1 medium onion, finely chopped
1 garlic clove, finely chopped
grated zest of 1 orange
juice of 1 orange
2 tablespoons chopped parsley
1 teaspoon chopped fresh thyme
2 teaspoons chopped fresh sage
salt and freshly ground pepper
6 slices of bacon

Place the duck pieces and belly of pork in a roasting pan and cook in a preheated oven at 425°F for 15 minutes. (This makes it easier to cut the duck breast meat into strips and to cut the leg meat and pork into chunks so that they can be coarsely ground.) Immerse the duck and chicken livers in boiling water for 2–3 minutes, then drain. Allow the meats and livers to cool. Mix together the port, red wine and crushed juniper berries. Add the strips of breast meat and leave to marinate overnight in the refrigerator.

The next day, coarsely grind the leg meat (discarding most of the duck skin), the pork and livers. Add the onion and garlic to the ground meat mixture, then add the orange zest and juice, parsley, thyme, sage and salt and pepper to taste. Mix thoroughly. Line a 2-pound terrine or loaf pan with the flattened and stretched slices of bacon, letting them hang over the rim of the pan. Put in a layer of the ground meat mixture, then some strips of duck breast. Add more of the ground meat mixture and then another layer of duck breast. Continue layering until the ingredients are used up. Pour over the marinade and fold the bacon over the top. Cover the terrine with aluminum foil and stand the dish in a roasting pan of hot water. Cook in a preheated oven at 325°F for 1½–2 hours. Remove from the oven and press down with weights while cooling. Refrigerate until needed, and cut into slices to serve.

JP

Rabbit and Beer Terrine

Owing to the sentimentalization of rabbits in the media, tons of this good and by anyone's standards healthy meat is dumped each year. Rabbit is excellent eating and this pleasant terrine makes fine picnic material.

2 pounds boned rabbit
1 pound belly of pork, boned and skinned
1¼ cups beer
1 bay leaf
fresh thyme and parsley
salt and freshly ground pepper
½ pound thin slices of bacon

Marinate the rabbit and pork in the beer, herbs, salt and pepper overnight. Drain, reserving the marinade. Grind the meats separately. Line a terrine with the bacon slices. Layer the meat in the terrine in alternate layers. Pour in the marinade. Cover tightly and bake in a preheated oven at 300°F for 2½–3 hours, until firm to the touch. Keep for a day or two to mature before serving.

CDW

Welsh Lamb Pie

Hurrah for Wales, home of the best spring lamb! In the words of an old rhyme: "Oh the mountain sheep were sweeter, but the valley sheep were fatter, so we gobbled up the former and we drove away the latter." This pie is best made with hill lamb and baby carrots and is very good.

1½ pounds neck of lamb
¼ cup chopped onion
salt and freshly ground pepper
1 pound refrigerated ready-made pie crust
1 cup sliced carrots
1 teaspoon chopped parsley
beaten egg to glaze

Remove all the bones from the lamb and dice the meat; set aside. Put the bones in a saucepan and add the onion, water to cover and a seasoning of salt and pepper. Bring to the boil, then simmer for 1½ hours. Strain the stock.

Line a pie dish with half of the pastry. Put in the diced lamb, carrots and parsley and season with salt and pepper. Cover with the remaining pastry, and seal and flute the edge. Make a small hole in the center of the pastry lid. Brush with beaten egg, then bake in a preheated oven at 350°F for 2 hours or until the pastry is golden brown. Pour the stock through the hole in the lid, adding enough to fill the pie, and leave to cool before serving.

CDW

Cornish Pasties

Many years ago I had a criminal law tutor who was a Cornish druid. He was a fascinating man and, as we often traveled the same subway route, I would talk to him about things Cornish. I believe I still have life membership of *Mebyon Kernow*, the Cornish Nationalist Party, as a result. His name was Mr Treleven (such was the formality of the day that I never knew his Christian name) and he gave me his mother's recipe for pasties, admonishing me never to put carrot into them as this was a blasphemy. He also told me that a pasty without potatoes is a "hoggan" and a "tiddy oggy" with them. So, dear Mr Treleven, wherever you are, thank you, and no doubt your lectures helped keep me out of prison too.

Makes 8

FOR THE PASTRY:
1 pound all-purpose flour
pinch of salt
½ cup solid vegetable shortening
1¼ cups cold water
½ cup lard
beaten egg or milk to glaze

FOR THE FILLING:
2 pounds rump or topside of beef, finely diced
2 cups diced potatoes
1 cup chopped onions
½ teaspoon dried thyme
salt and freshly ground pepper

To make the pastry, sift the flour and salt into a bowl and cut the shortening until the mixture resembles coarse bread crumbs. Bind to a stiff dough with as much of the cold water as required. Roll out the dough to an oblong. Dot with small pieces of one-quarter of the lard, then fold the dough into three, as for flaky or puff pastry. Roll out again, dot with another quarter of the lard and fold in three. Roll out and fold two more times, dotting with the remaining lard.

Mix all the filling ingredients together and season well.

Roll out the pastry dough ¼-inch thick and cut into eight rounds, each 6 inches in diameter. Divide the filling among the rounds. Dampen the edges and draw them together at the top. Crimp the edges firmly together to seal, and make a small slit to allow the steam to escape. Brush the pasties with beaten egg or milk, then bake in a preheated oven at 350°F for about 45 minutes or until golden.

CDW

Raised Tongue Pie

Raised pies hold so many memories for me: childhood point to points, shooting picnics, racing picnics with... Ah well, leave that for the tabloids. There was also the ridiculous occasion when we were shooting at Highgrove and Jennifer said, "I could eat a horse." I replied, "Well, it's just as well, as I've bought some horse pies." We had such wonderful hysterics of laughter after this that they had to delay filming for 15 minutes. This is a very good picnic pie. The best stock for the filling is made from pig's trotters as it is good and stiff; the least good is from stock cubes with added gelatin.

FOR THE HOT WATER CRUST PASTRY:
1 pound all-purpose flour
3 teaspoons salt
1 cups lard
1¼ cups hot water

2 pounds ox tongue, cooked
½ pound veal or pork loose sausagemeat
½ teaspoon each ground mace and cayenne pepper
salt and freshly ground pepper
6 ounces bacon slices
beaten egg to glaze
1¼ cups jellied stock, heated

To make the pastry, sift the flour and salt into a warm bowl and make a well in the center. In a saucepan heat the lard in the water until melted. Pour into the well in the flour and mix quickly together with a wooden spoon. When the mixture is cool enough to handle, knead it until all the flour is worked in and the dough is smooth and free from cracks. Use at once.

Using three-quarters of the pastry dough, mold the dough by hand to make a round, deep-sided pie shell. The walls of the case should be approximately ⅓ inch thick. Leave to cool. Roll up the piece of tongue and put it into the pie shell, curling it round to fit in. Fill the spaces with the sausagemeat, and season with the mace, cayenne pepper, salt and pepper. Cover with bacon slices.

Make a lid with the remaining pastry dough and put it in place, sealing the edge. Make a small hole in the center of the lid. Brush with beaten egg, then bake in a preheated oven at 425°F for 30 minutes. Turn down the heat to 325°F and bake for a further 2 hours. Allow the pie to cool slightly before pouring in the heated jellied stock through the hole in the pastry lid. Leave to cool completely before cutting.

Ham and Celeriac Salad

A lovely comforting salad for a picnic, this is much loved by border poachers and reivers. This is as made by my friend Isabel Rutherford.

1 pound celeriac
1 fresh tart apple
juice of 1 lemon
salt and freshly ground pepper
2 tablespoons strong English mustard
1¼ cups mayonnaise
1 celery heart, finely diced
½ pound good cooked ham, thickly sliced from the bone

Coarsely grate the celeriac and apple into lemon juice, tossing frequently to prevent discoloration. Season, then add the mustard, mayonnaise, diced celery and ham. Mix well.

CDW

Tabboule Salad

You can eat Tabboule in your fingers if you are an experienced Middle-Eastern eater; otherwise take forks along.

½ cup bulghur wheat
4 whole scallions, finely chopped
4 heaping tablespoons chopped parsley
3 tablespoons chopped fresh mint
salt and freshly ground pepper
4 tablespoons olive oil
juice of 1 small lemon
2 tomatoes, peeled and chopped

Put the bulghur in a sieve and rinse well, then leave to soak in cold water to cover for 30 minutes. Drain well and squeeze dry. Put the bulghur in a bowl and add the scallions, squeezing them with the bulghur to release their juices. Add the parsley, mint, salt and pepper. Add the olive oil and lemon juice and toss together thoroughly. Leave in a cool place for a short while to allow the flavors to mingle. Add the chopped tomatoes just before serving. I sometimes add a little diced cucumber, but this too should be added just before serving as the liquid given off by the cucumber can spoil the texture of the salad.

JP

Illustrated overleaf

Barbecued Oysters

Four years ago I went camping with my schoolfriend Christine, her husband Douglas and my beloved godson, David Wain-Heapy. We camped just across the estuary from the Belon oyster beds in Brittany, and it was there that David discovered a passion for oysters almost equal to my own. As up until then his food interests had been somewhat limited, I was overjoyed. He is now a connoisseur of a good oyster. We had many barbecues and, as we didn't have a proper oyster knife, this is one of the things we learned to do.

6 oysters per person
fresh lemon juice

Place your oysters on your barbecue or fire and leave them until they just open. They taste wonderful, and a squeeze of lemon is the most you need for seasoning. Even people who are not fond of raw oysters enjoy them this way.

CDW

Index